The Golden Age
Of Children's
Book Illustration

W.H.R.

The Golden Age of
CHILDREN'S BOOK
ILLUSTRATION

RICHARD DALBY

Michael O'Mara Books Limited

First published in 1991 by Michael O'Mara Books Limited,
9 Lion Yard, Tremadoc Road, London SW4 7NQ, UK

Visit our website at www.mombooks.com

A CIP catalogue record for this book is available from the British Library

ISBN 1-85479-796-4

ACKNOWLEDGEMENTS

The publishers gratefully acknowledge permission given by the following to
reproduce illustrations and would be pleased to hear from copyright holders
whom they have been unable to trace:
Chris Beetles, St James's, London (Louis Wain and Margaret Tarrant);
Curtis Brown (E.H. Shepard);
E.T. Archive (Edward Dalziel and Edward J. Detmold);
Gallery Children's Books, an imprint of East-West Publications (UK) Ltd
    (H. Willebeek Le Mair © Soefi Stichting Inayat Fundatie Sirdar);
Peter Newark's Western Americana (Maxfield Parrish);
Laurence Pollinger Ltd (W. Heath Robinson ©
    The Estate of Mrs J.C. Robinson);
Frederick Warne (Beatrix Potter)

Designed by James Campus

Typesetting: Florencetype Ltd, Kewstoke, Avon
Printed and bound in China

CONTENTS

INTRODUCTION

THE origins of what has come to be known as the Golden Age of children's book illustration can be traced back to the work of George Cruikshank, now recognized as the first artist to set a standard and form in children's book illustration. Working in the early part of the nineteenth century, he laid the framework for the great flowering of the illustrator's art that began in the mid-nineteenth century. His genius directly inspired Richard Doyle and John Tenniel, while the pioneering work of the Victorian engravers William James Linton and the Dalziel brothers and of the colour printer Edmund Evans contributed greatly to the enduring success of Walter Crane, Randolph Caldecott, Kate Greenaway and Beatrix Potter. With these illustrators, nursery rhymes, fairy tales, animal stories and children's picture books entered upon a new and 'modern' era of artistic refinement.

The last years of the nineteenth century saw a great awakening of interest in folk tales, revived by Andrew Lang and Joseph Jacobs, and in the pages of the *Strand* magazine, from all parts of the world. At the same time Howard Pyle was revolutionizing American children's books, and encouraging his many talented students to follow his example. This revival in the appreciation of old fairy tales and children's stories coincided with the threat to traditional cultures posed by the advance of the industrial world.

The Golden Age of children's book illustration reached its undoubted peak in the decade from 1905 to 1914 when dozens of opulent large quarto gift books with mounted colour plates, and hundreds of cheaper but often equally beautiful illustrated volumes were published every year. These years saw the rise of this century's greatest and most popular illustrators, including Arthur Rackham, Edmund Dulac, Willy Pogany, Kay Nielsen, Edward J. Detmold, W. Heath Robinson and Jessie Willcox Smith. This incredible wealth of talent of book illustration, the innumerable fine drawings and paintings combining fantasy, humour and sheer beauty, and the array of masterly pictorial cover designs richly adorned in gilt have never been equalled.

Although the overall quality of book production never recovered its former grandeur after the First World War, Arthur Rackham and many of his younger contemporaries helped to sustain the Golden Age during the 1920s and 1930s. Among the most stunning volumes which retained all the glory of the pre-war years were Harry Clarke's *The Fairy Tales of Perrault* (1922), William M. Timlin's *The Ship That Sailed to Mars* (1923), and Edward J. Detmold's *The Arabian Nights* (1924).

The death of Rackham and the appearance of his last superb book illustrations in *The Wind in the Willows*, coinciding with the start of the Second World War, marked the final demise of the Golden Age.

GEORGE CRUIKSHANK

1792–1878

It is now generally agreed that the Golden Age of children's book illustration may be conveniently dated from the first English translation of the Grimm Brothers' *German Popular Stories* (two volumes, 1823–6) with pictures by George Cruikshank. Unlike the static set pieces found in earlier book illustrations, Cruikshank's detail faithfully followed the text, the Gothic liveliness of his design matched the spirit of the tales perfectly, and his exuberant vitality filled every corner of the pictures. His 22 drawings for these fairy tales became extremely popular, and they remain inextricably linked with the stories.

John Ruskin considered them 'unrivalled in masterfulness of touch since Rembrandt, and in some qualities of delineation unrivalled even by him'. The ultimate praise came from the brothers themselves when they insisted that Cruikshank's illustrations should be used in later editions of the book.

After illustrating a large number of books, including *Oliver Twist* (1838), Cruikshank achieved a huge and unexpected success with *The Bottle*, a series of eight plates demonstrating the inexorable consequences of alcohol from conviviality to madness. After many years of hard drinking, he was now converted to total abstinence. This theme was clearly evident in his controversial new versions of traditional fairy tales, where he illustrated and rewrote four famous stories: *Hop o'my Thumb* (1853), *Jack and the Beanstalk* (1854), *Cinderella and the Glass Slipper* (1854), and *Puss in Boots* (1864).

Several critics and former colleagues, including Charles Dickens, reproached Cruikshank for altering the texts of these classic tales in his 'Fairy Library', but the illustrations survived the test of time and the four volumes were reissued in a special one-volume edition in 1885.

9

RICHARD DOYLE

1824–1883

Richard Doyle was one of the most popular Victorian illustrators of fairy stories, and the earliest natural successor to George Cruikshank. As a boy he was captivated by the 'St George and the dragon' theme, and became regarded as the supreme master of dragon illustrations, besides those of giants, pixies, witches and nature spirits. He loved collecting obscure foreign folk legends, especially those featuring strange and supernatural creatures.

He inherited his gifts from his father, John Doyle, a notable political caricaturist widely known as 'H.B.'. Richard ('Dickie') had no art training outside his father's studio, but always possessed an extraordinary power of fanciful and imaginative draughtsmanship and sense of the grotesque. His boyhood fascination with fairy stories stayed with him all his life, and stimulated his greatest book illustrations.

Doyle joined the staff of *Punch* at the age of 19 in 1843 and designed the cover picture which was used for more than a century. After resigning from *Punch* seven years later he concentrated mainly on book illustration and watercolour painting.

He collaborated with John Leech, W. C. Stanfield and other artists on the illustrations for three of Dickens's Christmas books: *The Chimes* (1844), *The Cricket on the Hearth* (1845), and *The Battle of Life* (1846).

In 1846 Doyle first made his name as an important fairy tale illustrator with his drawings for *The Fairy Ring*, a new translation of Grimm's popular tales. His illustrations in this volume were considered by some critics, including W. M. Thackeray, to rival those of Cruikshank, hitherto the acknowledged master of the genre.

This was followed by the tremendously successful *Fairy Tales from All Nations* (1849) compiled by 'Anthony R. Montalbà' (i.e., Anthony Whitehill), with 12 wood-engraved plates and 12 other illustrations by Doyle. The stories were later reissued separately as *Snow-White and Rosy-Red*, *The Enchanted Crow*, *Fortune's Favourite*, and *The Feast of the Dwarfs*. The artist was able to indulge his devotion to fairy tale mythology with his many drawings and vignettes of elves, pixies, and mythical creatures, forming elaborate initials or decorating the borders on each page.

Some of Doyle's best designs were published in his *Juvenile Calendar and Zodiac of Flowers* (1849) and were reprinted in many later anthologies. Among his next book illustrations were Mark Lemon's *The Enchanted Doll* (1849); *The Story of Jack and the Giants* (1850); and John Ruskin's *The King of the Golden River* (1850), one of the earliest English examples of a fantasy written specifically for children. Enormously popular, it went through three editions during the first year of publication. Doyle's famous drawing of the South West Wind with the bugle-like nose was redrawn (with bulbous-shaped nose) for the third edition.

In his illustrations for *The Scouring of the White Horse* by Thomas Hughes (1858), Doyle was one of the first artists to parody antiquity for children, portraying his Saxon warriors as fat, jolly human beings instead of unreal historical heroes.

In 1865 Doyle illustrated J. R. Planché's retelling of the Sleeping Beauty story in *An Old Fairy Tale Told Anew*.

Richard Doyle's masterpiece is undoubtedly *In Fairyland, a series of Pictures from the Elf World* with a poem by William Allingham, printed by Edmund Evans and published by Longman shortly before Christmas 1869 (dated 1870). He was given a completely free hand in producing his most imaginative pictures – 16 colour plates with 36 illustrations and a pictorial title-page – for this glorious folio in decorated green cloth. The whole volume, which shows Doyle's secret fairy world at its most enchanting, is one of the finest examples of Victorian book production. In 1884 the illustrations for *In Fairyland* were adapted to be used with a specially written story, *The Princess Nobody, a Tale of Fairy Land* by Andrew Lang.

Richard Doyle died in London on 11 December 1883, survived by his artist brothers, James and Charles Doyle. The latter was the father of Arthur Conan Doyle, creator of the immortal Sherlock Holmes.

JOHN TENNIEL

1820–1914

Like Richard Doyle, his predecessor at *Punch*, John Tenniel was celebrated both as a major Victorian caricaturist and as a children's book illustrator. As *Alice in Wonderland*'s first and most famous illustrator, Tenniel entered into Lewis Carroll's imagination perfectly, and his drawings are still being reproduced in modern editions of this ageless classic.

John Tenniel was born in London on 28 February 1820. His early friendship with the artist Charles Keene developed a talent for scholarly caricature. In 1850 he was invited by Mark Lemon to fill the position of joint cartoonist (with John Leech) on *Punch*, in succession to Richard Doyle. When Leech died, Tenniel continued to work alone on the main weekly political cartoon. Before retiring in 1901 at the age of 81, Tenniel contributed around 2,300 cartoons to *Punch*, innumerable smaller drawings, double-page cartoons for *Punch's Almanac* and other special numbers, and 250 designs for *Punch's Pocket-books*.

He had a wonderful gift for observation, always drawing either from imagination or memory, never from models. His incredible output was performed with a single eye, the other having been lost during a fencing bout in his youth. He was knighted in 1893, following Gladstone's personal recommendation.

Tenniel's parallel career as a book illustrator began in 1846 with *Undine* and *Juvenile Verse and Picture Book*, followed by *Aesop's Fables* (1848, 100 drawings) and Moore's *Lalla Rookh* (1861, 69 drawings). He also contributed to the Dalziels' edition of the *Arabian Nights* (1863–5).

His association with 'Lewis Carroll' (Charles Dodgson) on *Alice* was always a difficult one, but open quarrels were generally avoided. He agreed to accept most of Carroll's demands and foibles, and was even persuaded (against his usual

practice) to draw Alice from a model – not the real Alice Liddell, but another little girl of similar appearance. Tenniel's Alice has often been described as a 'wax puppet' or miniature adult, rather than a child, but she still remains the universally accepted visual image, in spite of countless subsequent artists' interpretations during the present century.

It was Tenniel who was largely responsible for the suppression of the first edition of *Alice's Adventures in Wonderland* (dated 1865), being even more dissatisfied than Carroll with the printing of the pictures. This edition has become one of the most celebrated rarities in the antiquarian book world. The accepted edition (dated 1866) was published by Macmillan in November 1865 in time for the Christmas market.

In spite of their stormy relationship, Tenniel was the only artist Carroll wanted to illustrate the sequel volume, *Through the Looking Glass* (dated 1872). Tenniel was equally inspired in this book with his pictorial creation of Humpty Dumpty, Tweedledum and Tweedledee, and all Carroll's other much loved characters. He incorporated several political picture-jokes, such as turning Gladstone and Disraeli into the Lion and the Unicorn. (Tenniel himself was very like the White Knight in appearance.)

After 1872 Tenniel understandably refused to work with Carroll on his later books, tactfully explaining 'the faculty of making drawings for book illustration has departed from me'. In private he warned Harry Furniss (who illustrated the two *Sylvie and Bruno* books): 'Dodgson is impossible! You will never put up with that conceited old Don for more than a week!' (The other two notable illustrators of Carroll's humorous children's books were Henry Holiday (*The Hunting of the Snark*) and Arthur B. Frost (*Phantasmagoria*), who also collaborated on *Rhyme? and Reason?*)

Tenniel survived long enough to see *Alice's Adventures in Wonderland* go out of copyright in 1907 and the consequent plethora of other illustrated editions (by Charles Robinson, Arthur Rackham, Millicent Sowerby, Thomas Maybank, Mabel Lucie Attwell, and others). He died on 25 February 1914, shortly before his ninety-fourth birthday.

THE DALZIEL BROTHERS

The Dalziel brothers – George (1815–1902), Edward (1817–1905), John (1822–69) and Thomas (1823–1906) – were the leading English wood engravers of the mid-Victorian period. Their facility for engraving (cutting on wood, which superseded steel) their client-artists' drawings was much more elaborate than anything attempted in this medium before.

At their peak in the two decades 1855–75 they made blocks for many important illustrated books including Edward Lear's revised *Book of Nonsense* (1861), and engraved Tenniel's illustrations for *Alice's Adventures in Wonderland* (1865), Hughes's MacDonald drawings, and George Cruikshank's series of fairy stories.

In 1863–5 they prepared their own edition of *The Arabian Nights* 'with upward of two hundred illustrations by eminent artists'. These included Tenniel, Pinwell and Houghton, as well as Thomas and Edward Dalziel themselves (published by Ward Lock in two volumes, 1865; previously issued in parts).

When not engraving the works of other artists, Thomas illustrated an edition of *The Pilgrim's Progress* (1865), and George drew for several magazines (notably *Fun* and *Judy*) and *Hood's Comic Annual* later in his career.

In their eighties, Edward and George collaborated on a volume entitled *The Brothers Dalziel* (1901), a record of their distinguished career which had proved so invaluable to the leading book illustrators of the nineteenth century.

ARTHUR HUGHES

1832–1915

As Tenniel is irrevocably linked with Lewis Carroll, so Arthur Hughes will always be closely associated with the children's books of George MacDonald.

Hughes was born in London on 27 January 1832. From 1847 he studied at the Royal Academy Schools where he befriended the young artists of the newly formed Pre-Raphaelite Brotherhood: J. E. Millais, Dante Gabriel Rossetti and William Holman Hunt. He was deeply influenced by their ideas and approach to black and white illustration, and worked alongside Millais and Rossetti in his first book commission, William Allingham's *The Music Master* in 1855.

He also collaborated with other artists on the first illustrated edition of *Tom Brown's Schooldays* (1869), *Mother Goose's National Nursery Rhymes* (1870–1), and *Christmas Carols* (1874).

His partnership with George MacDonald began with the collection of stories, *Dealings with the Fairies* (1867). He then illustrated the author's *At the Back of the North Wind* (serialized in *Good Words for the Young*, 1868; book 1871), followed by *Ronald Bannerman's Boyhood* (1871), *The Princess and the Goblin* (1871), *Gutta Percha Willie* (1873), and the new edition of *Phantastes: a Faerie Romance* (1905). Hughes's illustrations convey the sense of magic and lyrical quality of MacDonald's writing perfectly. Hughes also illustrated three children's books by Greville MacDonald (George's son): *The Magic Crook* (1911), *Trystie's Quest* (1912), and *Jack and Jill* (1913).

Forrest Reid wrote of Hughes's mind 'hovering perpetually on the border line between sleeping and waking, vision and reality: when the dream world overlaps the real world then the adventure begins.' He died at Kew Green on 22 December 1915.

18

EDWARD LEAR

1812–1888

Manypeeplia Upsidownia

In his role as the 'Old Derry Down Derry, who loved to see little folks merry', Lear's spirited drawings to his farcical nonsense rhymes, full of movement but deceptively simple, had an enormous appeal for the Victorian child, still bound by the restraints of the time. Beset by improving tales, they loved the comic and lively world of the Young Lady of Norway, the Young Person of Smyrna, the Old Man with a Beard, and all the other limerick characters. Although his nonsense drawings have a childish spontaneity, they also have the controlled line of the practised draughtsman – who was invited to give art lessons to Queen Victoria!

Edward Lear was born in Holloway, north London, on 12 May 1812, the sickly twentieth child of a London stockbroker. He displayed an early talent for drawing flowers, butterflies and birds, and his first book, *Illustrations for the Family of the Psittacidae*, was published when he was 19.

While Lear was employed to draw the animals in Lord Derby's impressive menagerie and aviary at Knowsley Hall, he amused the Lord's grandchildren in the nursery by drawing strange birds and people accompanied by humorous verses. Greeted 'with uproarious delight' by all who read the manuscript, Lear eventually decided to publish *The Book of Nonsense* in 1846 (originally under the pseudonym 'Derry Down Derry'; and further enlarged in 1861 under his own name).

Nonsense Songs, Stories, Botany and Alphabets was published in 1870 (dated 1871), containing the legendary 'Owl and the Pussycat' for the first time, together with 'The Jumblies' (who went to sea in a sieve) and many more of his delightful creatures. Charles Kingsley declared that this book 'has more wisdom and genius in it than all that [the philosophers] Bain and Spencer ever wrote'.

More Nonsense followed in 1871 (dated 1872); and his fourth collection, *Laughable Lyrics*, which introduced 'The Dong with the Luminous Nose' and 'The Pobble who had no Toes', was published in 1877.

Edward Lear died at his San Remo home on 29 January 1888, a few months after the death of Foss, his beloved 'cat who has no end of a tail', who had been his constant companion for many years.

C was a lovely Pussy Cat; its eyes were large & pale;
And on its back it had some stripes,
and several on his tail.

20

ELEANOR VERE BOYLE ('E.V.B.')

1825–1916

Eleanor Gordon was born in Auchlunies (Kincardineshire, Scotland), and married the Rev. Richard Boyle in 1845. She was taught and encouraged by the eminent artists Sir William Boxall, RA, and Sir Charles Eastlake, PRA; and from 1851 she illustrated several popular children's books under the initials 'E.V.B.'. These include *Child's Play* (1852), *A Children's Summer* (1853), Tennyson's *The May Queen* (1861), *Woodland Gossip* (1864), Carové's *Story Without an End* (1868), *A Dream Book* (1870), Andersen's *Fairy Tales* (1872), *Beauty and the Beast* (1875), Keary's *The Magic Valley* (1877), *A New Child's Play* (1877), *A Book of the Heavenly Birthdays* (1894), *A Garden of Pleasure* (1895), and *Peacock's Pleasaunce* (1908).

She remained one of the foremost practitioners in the art of depicting coy, demure little children, much in vogue with the comfortable Victorian middle class, for over half a century. In her later years she published several books on gardens and flowers. She died in Brighton in 1916.

WALTER CRANE

1845–1915

As the earliest successful exponent of the colour picture book, Walter Crane played an invaluable part in the development of children's book illustration, and was among the first artists to acknowledge the visual unity of the double-page spread. In identifying the special appeal of children's books he wrote: 'They are attractive to designers of an imaginative tendency, for in a sober and matter-of-fact age they afford perhaps the only outlet for unrestrained flights of fancy open to the modern illustrator, who likes to revolt against the despotism of facts.'

He was born in Liverpool on 15 August 1845, the son of portrait miniaturist Thomas Crane. At the age of 14 he drew some coloured page designs for Tennyson's *Lady of Shalott* which clearly demonstrated his love of old illuminated books with their union of the calligrapher's and the decorator's art.

An early devotee of the Pre-Raphaelites and the teachings of John Ruskin, Crane was apprenticed to William James Linton, the eminent engraver whom Rossetti preferred to the Dalziel brothers. In Linton's studio he had ample opportunity to study the contemporary artists (notably Tenniel, Millais and Rossetti) whose work passed through his hands.

In 1865 Crane began illustrating a series of sixpenny toybooks of nursery rhymes for the colour printer Edmund Evans, and the newly established publisher Frederick Warne. Among the first titles were *The House that Jack Built*, *The History of Cock Robin*, *Sing a Song of Sixpence*, *The Railroad Alphabet* and *The Farmyard ABC*. These represented the first successful attempt to mass-produce well-drawn, designed and printed books in colour for young children, and established Crane's reputation as the leading 'nursery illustrator'.

Between 1867 and 1876 Crane designed and illustrated nearly forty more of

22

these toybooks for George Routledge (Warne's brother-in-law), all lovingly printed by Evans. Though Crane was initially limited to the use of three colours, these books clearly showed his genius as a draughtsman. The most popular titles included *I Saw Three Ships*, *Goody Two Shoes*, *The Fairy Ship*, *The Frog Prince*, *Cinderella*, *Beauty and the Beast*, *Jack and the Beanstalk*, *Puss-in-Boots*, *This Little Pig*, *The Three Bears*, and the educational titles *Grammar in Rhyme* and *Multiplication Table in Verse*.

Several of Crane's illustrations, like those in *The Fairy Ship*, showed the influence of Japanese art and colour prints. He later wrote about these: 'Their treatment, in definite block outline and flat, brilliant, as well as delicate colours, struck me at once and I endeavoured to apply these methods to the modern fanciful and humorous subjects of the children's toybooks and the methods of wood-engraving and machine printing.' He was always concerned that the text should be harmonized and integrated completely with the illustration, which in turn must fill the whole frame of the page.

In 1876 he collaborated with Kate Greenaway in *The Quiver of Love: a collection of Valentines, Ancient and Modern*; and with John Tenniel and other artists in *Mother Goose's Nursery Rhymes and Fairy Tales*.

Crane's most ambitious and popular titles to date were the two songbooks, *The Baby's Opera* (1877) and *The Baby's Bouquet* (1879), where the music was perfectly worked into the decorative scheme. Besides designing the entire volumes, he calligraphed the whole text, humorously incorporating the hieroglyph of a crane that acted as his signature to every picture. (The title-page of *The Baby's Opera* is a theatre stage, with the crane's head peeping around the corner of the curtain!) With *The Baby's Own Aesop* (1887), the three titles were published together as *Triplets* in 1889. Another Crane trilogy comprised *Slateandpencilvania* (1885), *Little Queen Anne* (1886) and *Pothooks and Perseverance* (1886), published together as *The Romance of the Rs* (1886).

The First of May: A Fairy Masque (by John R. Wise, 1881), with text and decorations reproduced by photogravure, was one of Crane's most beautiful and expensive productions. In 1882 he illustrated his sister Lucy's translation of

23

"No, Master," said Puss, "give me boots to my
feet—
A pair of top-boots—and please leave me alive,
And you shall just see how we'll flourish and
thrive."

Household Stories from Grimm. The 'Goose Girl' picture from this volume was reproduced in tapestry by William Morris, and is now in the Victoria and Albert Museum.

Walter Crane also illustrated sixteen books by the popular children's writer, Mrs Molesworth, running annually from *Tell Me a Story* (1875), *Carrots* (1876), *The Cuckoo Clock* (1877), *Grandmother Dear* (1878), *The Tapestry Room* (1879), through to *The Rectory Children* (1889) and *The Children of the Castle* (1890).

Among the many other children's books decorated and illustrated by Crane were Mary de Morgan's *The Necklace of Princess Florimunde* (1880), Theo Marzials' *Pan Pipes: a Book of Old Songs* (1883), J. M. D. Meiklejohn's *The Golden Primer* (1884–5), Oscar Wilde's *The Happy Prince and Other Tales* (1888), *Flora's Feast: a Masque of Flowers* (1889), *Queen Summer* (1892), Nathaniel Hawthorne's *Wonder Book for Boys and Girls* (1892), Margaret Deland's *The Old Garden* (1893), *A Floral Fantasy in an Old English Garden* (1898), *A Flower Wedding, Described by Two Wallflowers* (1905), and *Flowers from Shakespeare's Garden* (1906). For the adult market the finest of Crane's book illustrations appeared in Edmund Spenser's *The Faerie Queene* (1894–6) and *The Shepheard's Calendar* (1898).

The Walter Crane Readers, first published in 1898–9, remained in general use for nearly forty years, and exercised wide influence on the careers of many artists and illustrators during that period.

Crane was associated with William Morris and the socialist movement for many years, and devoted much time and energy to the Art Workers' Guild, aiming to bring art into the daily life of all classes. He designed socialist posters with 'Leisure for All' and 'The Land for the People' banners.

He died on 14 March 1915.

KATE GREENAWAY

1846–1901

In the portrayal of childhood, no Victorian artist could combine charm, beauty and gentleness with such style as Kate Greenaway, the undisputed queen of nursery books. Her mob-capped little girls and frilly-trousered, short-jacketed boys inhabited an idyllic Gainsborough-inspired rural paradise. Her quaint costume designs so captivated the public in Britain, Europe and America, that it was claimed 'Kate Greenaway dressed the children of two continents'.

She was born in London on 17 March 1846, daughter of the wood-engraver John Greenaway. She studied at Heatherley's and under Legros at the Slade School. Her first book illustration was a frontispiece for William Kingston's *Infant Amusements, or How to Make a Nursery Happy* (1867), a prophetic title which aptly summed up all her future artwork. In 1870 she illustrated *Aunt Louisa's London Toy Books: Diamonds and Toads* for Frederick Warne, the publisher who was to reissue most of her best-loved books at the turn of the century.

During the 1870s Kate Greenaway drew for several important magazines, including *Little Folks*, *St. Nicholas*, the *Graphic*, and the *Illustrated London News*. She also received several book commissions from the publishers Griffith & Farran, including *Fairy Gifts or a Wallet of Wonders* (1874), Kathleen Knox's *Seven Birthdays, A Fairy Chronicle* (1876), and Fanny Lablanche's *Starlight Stories Told to Bright Eyes and Listening Ears* (1877).

Kate Greenaway worked extremely hard, almost to the point of exploitation, for the firm of Marcus Ward, for whom she designed many greeting cards and calendars, besides a dozen books, including Rosa Mulholland's *Puck and Blossom* (1874), Miranda Hill's *The Fairy Spinner* (1875), and *The Quiver of Love, a collection of Valentines* (1876) in collaboration with Walter Crane.

K.G.

KATE GREENAWAY

In 1877 Kate Greenaway filled a notebook with nearly fifty pages of drawings and verses, and presented them to her father. He showed them to Edmund Evans, the most celebrated Victorian printer of children's books in colour (notably Doyle's *In Fairyland*). Evans found these designs delightfully natural and spontaneous, and determined to publish them in book form in association with George Routledge. *Under the Window* appeared in time for Christmas 1878, and was an immediate triumph.

Kate Greenaway's Birthday Book for Children was published in 1880, containing 12 colour and over 350 tiny black and white illustrations, accompanied by Mrs Sale Barker's verses. Her next assignment was the equally pretty small-format volume, *Mother Goose or The Old Nursery Rhymes* (1881).

KATE GREENAWAY

Her intense love of flowers and gardens was given free rein in her next three books: *A Day in a Child's Life* (1881) is a delightful celebration of children in music and pictures, compared by some critics to the work of Botticelli and the flower paintings of the meticulous Dutch master, Van Huysam. *Language of Flowers* (1884) is considered by many to be the loveliest Greenaway book of all, the flowers and fruit here being seen as 'the highest point of her art'. Half of the first edition of 19,500 copies went immediately to America, where many collectors had them bound in leather and gold. *Marigold Garden* (1885) is said to have been Kate Greenaway's own favourite among all her own books. It was praised for its beauty of colour and freshness of design. She was now at the pinnacle of her success, with the Greenaway 'cult' reaching its height. A plethora of Greenaway artefacts such as dolls, wallpaper, fabrics, christening sets and fashions were manufactured in England and on the Continent.

Among her next books were *Kate Greenaway's Alphabet* (1885), *A Apple Pie* (1886), *Queen Victoria's Jubilee Garland* (1887), and *Kate Greenaway's Book of Games* (1889) describing 53 games with 24 illustrations in colour.

During the 1880s the most successful of her book illustrations which accompanied texts by other authors were Jane and Ann Taylor's *Little Ann, and Other Poems* (1883; these verses had been Kate Greenaway's favourite childhood reading); Bret Harte's *The Queen of the Pirate Isle* (1886); Robert Browning's *The Pied Piper of Hamelin* (1888; one of her best-known and most rewarding works); and Beatrice Cresswell's *The Royal Progress of King Pepito* (1889).

Routledge also published the very popular *Kate Greenaway Almanack* every year from 1883 to 1895. Comprising around eight to ten pages, and measuring 3 in × 2 in, these miniature books featured some of her most accomplished work. English sales of the *Almanack* were exceeded by those in America, where demand for her books was immense. After a gap, Dent issued the final *Kate Greenaway's Almanack and Diary for 1897*.

She died at her home in Frognal, Hampstead, on 6 November 1901, just as her most accomplished successor as 'queen of the nursery books', Beatrix Potter, was launching her career with *Peter Rabbit*.

RANDOLPH CALDECOTT

1846–1886

Randolph Caldecott's name is often linked with those of Walter Crane and Kate Greenaway, forming the triumvirate of illustrators who began the new era of picture books for children in the 1870s. However Caldecott's sixteen immortal picture books are quite different to the more static, decorative work of Crane and Greenaway. He used very little detail, achieving his effect with the fewest possible strokes, and was deceptively subtle in his use of colour. His skill lay in sketching minutely observed scenes of everyday events, animals, and people full of the joy of living.

Caldecott was born in Chester on 22 March 1846, only five days after the birth of Kate Greenaway and barely seven months after Walter Crane. By the age of 6 he was drawing animals, both modelling them in clay and carving them out of wood.

While working as a bank clerk in his teens, he spent his spare time wandering and drawing in the countryside, fishing, shooting, and visiting fairs and markets – all future subjects for his picture books.

He then spent five years in Manchester (1867–72), studying at the School of Art. After several contributions to the *London Society* magazine, his first commissioned book illustrations appeared in Blackburn's *The Harz Mountains: A Tour in the Toy Country* (1873), followed by Louisa Morgan's *Baron Bruno . . . and other Fairy Stories* (1875), and Washington Irving's *Old Christmas* (1875) and *Bracebridge Hall* (1877).

Early in 1878 Caldecott began his fruitful association with Edmund Evans on a series of shilling toybooks. The artist agreed to produce two books annually, beginning that year with *The House that Jack Built* and *The Diverting History*

30

of John Gilpin. The first printing of 10,000 copies sold out very quickly, and Caldecott's success was assured.

The other Caldecott picture books are *The Babes in the Wood* and Goldsmith's *Elegy on the Death of a Mad Dog* (1879); *Sing a Song of Sixpence* and *Three Jovial Huntsmen* (1880); *The Farmer's Boy* and *The Queen of Hearts* (1881); *Hey Diddle Diddle, and Bye, Baby Bunting* and *The Milkmaid* (1882); *A Frog He Would A-Wooing Go* and *The Fox Jumps over the Parson's Gate* (1883); *Ride a Cock Horse to Banbury Cross,* and *a Farmer Went Trotting upon his Grey Mare* and *Come Lasses and Lads* (1884); Goldsmith's *Elegy on the Glory of Her Sex, Mrs. Mary Blaize* and *The Great Panjandrum Himself* (1885).

RANDOLPH CALDECOTT

These sixteen books won Caldecott international renown, earning him the description 'Lord of the Nursery'. He has been admired by many different artists from Van Gogh and Gauguin, who praised the life-like qualities of the ducks, geese and dogs in *John Gilpin*, to Maurice Sendak who has hailed the 'sense of music and dance' that characterizes Caldecott's picture books. Beatrix Potter had 'the greatest admiration for his work', and his influence is clearly seen both in her work and in that of Leslie Brooke (whose humorous pigs and other animals are almost identical to those in *Hey Diddle Diddle*).

Caldecott also illustrated several other children's books including Juliana Horatia Ewing's *Jackanapes* (1883), *Daddy Darwin's Dovecote* (1884) and *Lob Lie-by-the-Fire* (1885).

He sailed for Florida in October 1885, hoping to alleviate his failing health, but died there on 13 February 1886. His work is still greatly revered in America where the annual Caldecott Medal was inaugurated in 1938 to award the artist who has illustrated the 'most distinguished American picture book for children in the United States during the preceding year'.

E. V. BOYLE

plate 1

THE CATS HAVE COME TO TEA.

KATE GREENAWAY

plate 2

WISHES.

Oh, if you were a little boy,
    And I was a little girl—
Why you would have some whiskers grow
    And then my hair would curl.

Ah! if I could have whiskers grow,
    I'd let you have my curls;
But what's the use of wishing it—
    Boys never can be girls.

KATE GREENAWAY

plate 3

KATE GREENAWAY

plate 4

RANDOLPH CALDECOTT

plate 5

RANDOLPH CALDECOTT

plates 6 and 7

RANDOLPH CALDECOTT
plate 8

WALTER CRANE

plate 9

HELEN STRATTON

plate 10

HOWARD PYLE

plate 11

N. C. WYETH

plate 12

MAXFIELD PARRISH

plate 13

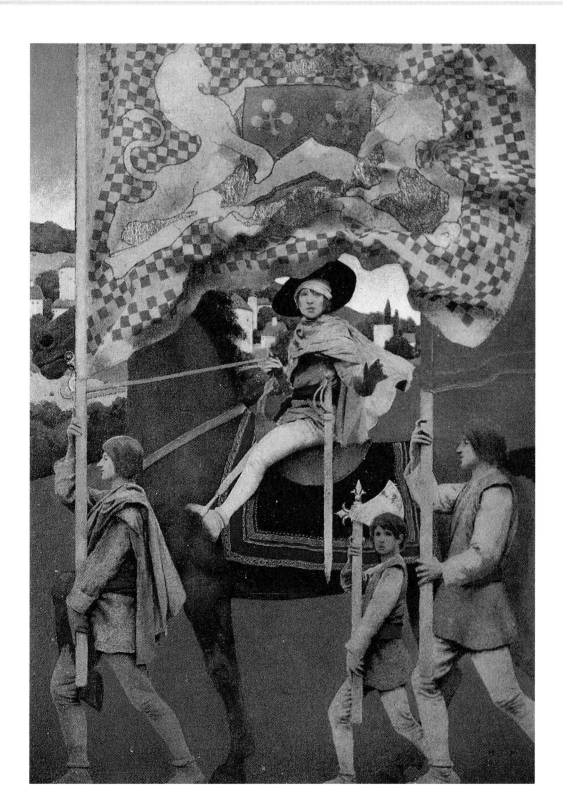

MAXFIELD PARRISH

plate 14

CHARLES ROBINSON

plate 15

H. M. BROCK

plate 16

JESSIE WILLCOX SMITH
plate 17

GORDON BROWNE

1858–1932

Gordon Browne was one of the greatest illustrators of the Golden Age, both in terms of quality and quantity. His sheer prolificity, averaging six books a year for nearly half a century, may have undervalued his reputation, but there is no doubt his innumerable vivid and painstakingly accurate drawings were always successful and much liked by generations of children addicted to the perennially popular classics he illustrated. Many late Victorian writers, from Mrs Ewing to Henty and Fenn, were delighted to have their stories illustrated by this most felicitous of artists.

GORDON BROWNE

He was born on 15 April 1858 at Banstead, Surrey, the son of Dickens' illustrator 'Phiz' – Hablot Knight Browne. His first book illustrations appeared in Ascott R. Hope's school story, *The Day After the Holidays* (1875). Early in his career he illustrated several juvenile books for Blackie, and contributed many drawings to *Chums* (including the original cover design), *Boy's Own Paper*, and many other magazines.

Among the many children's books he illustrated are *Hop o'my Thumb* (1886), *Beauty and the Beast* (1887), *Rip Van Winkle* (1887), Alice Corkran's *Down the Snow Stairs* (1887), Countess d'Aulnoy's *Fairy Tales* (1888), Andrew Lang's *Prince Prigio* (1889), *A Apple Pie* (1890), *National Rhymes for the Nursery* (1895), *Fairy Tales from Grimm* (1895), Harry Jones's *Prince Boohoo and Little Smuts* (1896), *The Surprising Adventures of Sir Toady Lion* (1897), *Dr Jollyboy's ABC* (1898), E. Nesbit's *The Story of the Treasure Seekers* (1899), F. W. Farrar's *Eric or Little by Little* (1899), Hans Andersen's *Fairy Tales* (1902), Tom Gallon's *The Charity Ghost* (1902), F. H. Darton's *Merry Tales of the Wise Men of Gotham* (1907), *Don Quixote* (1921), and over a hundred others.

He also drew more than five hundred illustrations for *The Henry Irving Shakespeare* (1895); and under the pseudonym 'A Nobody' he both wrote and illustrated *Nonsense for Somebody, Anybody and Everybody, Particularly the Baby-Body* (1895), *Some More Nonsense for the Same Bodies as Before* (1896) and *A Nobody's Scrapbook* (1899).

Browne died on 27 May 1932.

HOWARD PYLE

1853–1911

Howard Pyle was the great innovator who revolutionized American book illustration in the late nineteenth century. Before 1880 there were no American artists comparable to the great British illustrators. Apart from the artwork imported from Europe, the only outstanding book illustrations to be found in America were those done by artists who were, primarily, the leading painters of the day and occasionally 'lowered' themselves to undertake a few illustrations for a special book or magazine. Book illustration as an 'honourable' profession scarcely existed before Pyle's crusade to equal the best that Britain could offer. In less than thirty years, Howard Pyle not only created the Golden Age of American illustration, but also ensured that a large group of younger artists and disciples would carry on with similar work well into the twentieth century.

He was born at Wilmington, Delaware, on 5 March 1853. After attending the Art Students' League, New York, he first attracted attention by his line drawings in the style of Albrecht Dürer. He began contributing drawings of fables (signed 'H.P.') to the important children's magazine *St. Nicholas* soon after its inception in November 1873. After several book commissions including *Yankee Doodle* (1881), Tennyson's *Lady of Shalott* (1881), and James Baldwin's *Story of Siegfried* (1882), Howard Pyle made his debut as an author-illustrator with *The Merry Adventures of Robin Hood* (1883). He followed this with three collections of original short fairy tales, *Pepper & Salt, or Seasoning for Young Folk* (1886), *The Wonder Clock, or Four and Twenty Marvellous Tales* (1888), and *Twilight Land* (1895). These books displayed Pyle's devotion to medievalism, and his detailed concern with the total appearance of each book and page, though overall his decorations and design methods were not as elaborate as those pioneered by Walter Crane.

he Great Red Fox goes to call on neighbour Cock at his house because he will crow in the morn.

Equally popular were Pyle's two medieval novels, *Otto of the Silver Hand* (1888) and *Men of Iron* (1892); and a later historical work, *Jack Ballister's Fortunes* (1895), which covered another theme dear to Pyle's heart, pirates of the seventeenth and eighteenth centuries. (One of his posthumous collections was *Howard Pyle's Book of Pirates*, 1921.) Also in 1895 appeared Pyle's poignant fantasy on the meaning of life, *The Garden Behind the Moon*, inspired by the death of his son. Besides creating his own books, Pyle illustrated the works of many other authors including Van Dyke's *First Christmas Tree* (1897) and Deland's *Old Chester Tales* (1899).

His illustrations of American colonial life, particularly in New England and New Amsterdam, were highly acclaimed; and he also became prominent in decorative painting, 'The Landing of Carteret', and 'The Battle of Nashville' (for the capitol at St Paul, Minnesota), being among his best-known works.

In 1902 he began illustrating and writing his own version of the Arthurian legends, and these were published as *The Story of King Arthur and His Knights* (1903), *The Champions of the Round Table* (1905), *Sir Launcelot and His Companions* (1907), and *The Story of the Grail and the Passing of Arthur* (1910). Although Pyle's retelling of Malory's text is not always successful, the striking illustrations are among his best.

In the last year of his life Howard Pyle made his first and only visit to Europe, where he was taken ill, dying in Florence on 9 November 1911.

Through his unique gifts as a teacher of illustration, Howard Pyle bequeathed a wonderful legacy to his many followers. From 1894 he took classes at Philadelphia's Drexel Institute of Arts and Sciences, and in 1898 he established the Brandywine School of American illustration (situated by the Brandywine River near the Delaware/Pennsylvania border). Among the artists he taught and encouraged were several who were to become the greatest American book illustrators of the early twentieth century: N. C. Wyeth, Maxfield Parrish, Ethel Franklin Betts, and Jessie Willcox Smith who wrote that Howard Pyle 'simply blew away all that depressed atmosphere and made of art an entirely different thing'.

JESSIE WILLCOX SMITH

1863–1935

Pre-eminent among Howard Pyle's students was Jessie Willcox Smith, one of the most popular and best-known artists in America during the first thirty years of this century, still widely remembered alongside Charles Robinson and Kate Greenaway as a major illustrator of childhood.

Born on 6 September 1863, she studied drawing at the School of Design for Women in Philadelphia from 1885 to 1888, and her first published drawing appeared in *St. Nicholas* magazine in May 1988. In these early years her drawings followed the style of Kate Greenaway and the popular American illustrator Maud Humphrey, but after she joined Pyle's class at Drexel in 1894 her work matured and she steadily created more real-life children, each with distinct personalities.

Through Pyle's recommendation, Jessie Willcox Smith and fellow-student Violet Oakley were each commissioned to contribute five colour chromolithographs to the Houghton Mifflin edition of Longfellow's *Evangeline* (1897). In his introduction to the book Pyle wrote:

I do not know whether the world will find an equivalent pleasure to my own in the pictures that illustrate this book, for there is a singular delight in beholding the lucid thoughts of a pupil growing into form and color; the teacher enjoys a singular pleasure in beholding his instruction growing into a definite shape. Nevertheless, I venture to think that the drawings possess both grace and beauty.

The success of 'The Child', a calendar collaboration between Smith and Elizabeth Shippen Green, reissued as a volume *The Book of the Child* (1903), soon led to Jessie Willcox Smith's first book aimed specifically for children, the poetry compendium *Rhymes for Real Children*. Her next important book, Robert Louis

Stevenson's *A Child's Garden of Verses* (1905), was another important milestone in her career. One critic commented:

Miss Smith has created for us more of a type of childhood. There is no mistaking a drawing or painting by this artist: that charm in children that appeals to all pervades her work, and, although it is essentially illustrative in its rendering, a high order of craftsmanship is displayed. There is no better nor significant way to describe the irresistible charm of Miss Smith's work than to say its spirit is akin to that which pervades Stevenson's *A Child's Garden of Verses*.

Jessie Willcox Smith's series of illustrations featuring children at work and play continued with *Dream Blocks* (1908, by Aileen Higgins) and *The Seven Ages of Childhood* (1909, verses by Carolyn Wells), together with several editions compiled by the artist herself: *A Child's Book of Old Verses* (1910), *Dickens's Children* (1912), *The Little Mother Goose* (1915), and *A Child's Stamp Book of Old Verses* (1915).

JESSIE WILLCOX SMITH

The peak of her career was reached in 1916 with the beautiful series of plates for Charles Kingsley's *The Water Babies*, one of the most perfect combinations of pictures and prose in the Golden Age of book illustration. The complete set of these important paintings and decorations is preserved for posterity in the Library of Congress. Other popular classics illustrated in colour by Jessie Willcox Smith include Louisa May Alcott's *Little Women* (1915), George MacDonald's *At the Back of the North Wind* (1919) and *The Princess and the Goblin* (1920), and Johanna Spyri's *Heidi* (1922).

She continued her illustrated series for children in Nora A. Smith's *Boys and Girls of Bookland* (1923), and several anthologies by the sisters Ada and Eleanor Skinner: *A Child's Book of Modern Stories* (1920), *A Little Child's Book of Stories* (1922), *A Very Little Child's Book of Stories* (1923), and *A Child's Book of Country Stories* (1925). After this final title she retired from book illustration in order to concentrate wholly on portraiture and magazine covers.

From 1918 to 1933 Jessie Willcox Smith's paintings appeared monthly on the covers of *Good Housekeeping* magazine, all representing the image of America's ideal children at their most charming.

She died on 3 May 1935 at her home, Cogshill, near Philadelphia.

ETHEL FRANKLIN BETTS

Ethel Franklin Betts, a contemporary of Jessie Willcox Smith in Pyle's art class at the Drexel Institute, also became a very active and popular illustrator of children's books.

These included *Favorite Nursery Rhymes* (1906), *Familiar Nursery Jingles* (1908), *The Complete Mother Goose* (1909), *Fairy Tales from Grimm* (1909), Ingpen's *One Thousand Poems for Children* (1923), Burnett's *A Little Princess* (1937), and several books by the 'Hoosier Poet' James Whitcomb Riley: *The Raggedy Man* (1907), *While the Heart Beats Young* (1908), *The Orphant Annie Book* (1908), and *A Host of Children* (1920).

Her illustrations for the story 'The Six Swans' won a bronze medal at the Panama-Pacific International Exposition in 1915.

Among the other talented women artists and book illustrators whom Pyle taught at Drexel and the Brandywine School were Elizabeth Shippen Green, Elenore Plaisted Abbott, Violet Oakley, Waunita Smith, Alice Barber Stephens and Sara Stillwell.

MAXFIELD PARRISH

1870–1966

Maxfield Parrish was born in Philadelphia on 25 July 1870, son of artist Stephen Parrish. He attended the Pennsylvania Academy of Fine Arts, as well as studying under Howard Pyle at the Drexel Institute, and first became well known for his magazine cover designs (*Harper's Weekly*, *Century* magazine), later turning to posters, murals and other decorations.

By the turn of the century Parrish was becoming recognized as one of America's most successful artists, achieving national popularity for his distinctively elegant style, detailed backgrounds and glowing colours. The subtle shade of blue seen in many of his pictures came to be known as 'Maxfield Parrish blue'. Copies of his prints with the wonderful 'Parrish blue' sky could be found in countless nurseries and bedrooms across the land.

After illustrating L. Frank Baum's *Mother Goose in Prose* (1897), Parrish received several other book commissions including Kenneth Grahame's *The Golden Age* (1900) and *Dream Days* (1902). Describing the latter, Hubert von Herkomer (Slade Professor of Art at Oxford) wrote: 'Parrish has combined the photographic vision with the Pre-Raphaelite feeling . . . He can give suggestiveness without loss of unflinching detail. He has a strong sense of romance. He can be modern, medieval, or classic.'

Parrish's other books include Eugene Field's *Poems of Childhood* (1904), *The Arabian Nights* (1909), Hawthorne's *Wonder Book and Tanglewood Tales* (1910), and Palgrave's *Golden Treasury* (1911).

His poetic designs and fanciful pictures of a dream world always offered his admirers a soothing escape from reality.

He died on 30 March 1966 at his home in Plainfield, New Hampshire.

Maxfield Parrish.

N. C. WYETH

1882–1945

Newell Convers Wyeth studied at the Massachusetts Normal Art School before moving to Howard Pyle's Brandywine School of Illustration in 1902 at the age of 19. Wyeth had admired Pyle's work since childhood and he flourished in the dedicated and disciplined atmosphere of Pyle's school. In later years he acknowledged his debt to his mentor, remarking, 'Pyle emphasized that hard work, constantly applied, and the living of the simple life were two things that would bring about my making.' He learnt these lessons well, and went on to become the most prominent of Pyle's many distinguished students, and perhaps the greatest American illustrator of children's classics.

Having established his reputation providing illustrations for magazines and advertising material, Wyeth achieved his breakthrough into book illustration when he was asked to illustrate Robert Louis Stevenson's *Treasure Island* (1911) for the series 'Scribner's Illustrated Classics for Younger Readers'. Further commissions in this series included Stevenson's *Kidnapped* (1913) and *The Black Arrow* (1916), Malory's *Boy's King Arthur* (1917), Verne's *The Mysterious Island* (1918), Cooper's *Last of the Mohicans* (1919) and *The Deerslayer* (1925), and Kingsley's *Westward Ho!* (1920). Among the total of sixteen novels he illustrated for Scribner were several modern novels, including James Boyd's *Drums* (1928) and Marjorie Rawlings' *The Yearling* (1939); and for McKay he illustrated Creswick's *Robin Hood* (1917), Irving's *Rip Van Winkle* (1921) and Bulfinch's *Legends of Charlemagne* (1924).

Wyeth painted many fine pictures of frontier life in Colorado and New Mexico, and also lived for a time with the Indians in the West. He built up a large collection of costumes and props during his trips to the West which added

vital authenticity to his illustrations of both cowboys and Indians. This attention to detail extended beyond his own country and time. He rarely travelled far from home, preferring to exercise his powers of imagination, but his subjects were always thoroughly researched.

Wyeth lived out Pyle's principles of hard work and simple living in his own life, and passed on his ideals to his five children, all of whom became distinguished in their own fields. Childlike in his enthusiasm for life and the natural world around him, Wyeth was acutely sensitive to the individual needs and talents of his children. It is perhaps these qualities in his work that explain the universal popularity of his illustrations for children.

Wyeth rejoiced in his children's achievements, but sadly he did not live to see the full extent of their successes (his youngest son, Andrew Wyeth, is now widely regarded as the most popular painter in contemporary American art). N. C. Wyeth died in a tragic accident when the car in which he and his 4-year-old grandson were driving was struck by a train on a railroad crossing less than two miles from his home.

HENRY J. FORD

1860–1941

The name Henry J. Ford was familiar to countless children in the 1890s and beyond as the illustrator of Andrew Lang's cherished Fairy Books, published by Longman. The great success of these books was mainly due to the power of Ford's drawings and watercolours. Every year his seemingly inexhaustible imagination produced visions of demons and fairies, princes and princesses, animals and children, in these and many other books.

Born in London, Henry Justice Ford was one of seven brothers who all excelled at County cricket in the days of W. G. Grace. His eldest brother, William Justice Ford, was one of the greatest 'hitters' of the ball the world has ever seen, and the youngest, Francis Justice Ford, also achieved records at Lord's.

Henry was educated at Repton and acquired a First in Classics at Cambridge before entering the Slade to study under Alphonse Legros.

He began illustrating anthologies of children's fairy and folk tales and poetry in the late 1880s with *Aesop's Fables* (1888) and similar collections. His breakthrough came with *The Blue Fairy Book*, the first of Lang's twelve coloured fairy books, published in 1889, on which Ford collaborated with G. P. Jacomb-Hood.

Ford's widely imaginative graphic drawings, combining realism and fantasy, and full of action, complemented Lang's selection of fairy tales perfectly. In the later volumes Ford included a series of colour plates (in addition to the numerous black and white drawings) which strongly recalled Pre-Raphaelite paintings in their attention to detail and brilliant rosy colours. He was much influenced by his friend Sir Edward Burne-Jones in the dreamlike air of fantasy which pervades much of his work.

HENRY J. FORD

The Fairy Books continued to appear for twenty years and have been reprinted and enjoyed by successive generations ever since: *The Blue Fairy Book* (1889), *The Red Fairy Book* (1890, with Lancelot Speed), *The Green Fairy Book* (1892), *The Yellow Fairy Book* (1894), *The Pink Fairy Book* (1897), *The Grey Fairy Book* (1900), *The Violet Fairy Book* (1901), *The Crimson Fairy Book* (1903), *The Brown Fairy Book* (1904), *The Orange Fairy Book* (1906), *The Olive Fairy Book* (1907), and *The Lilac Fairy Book* (1910).

Ford also illustrated many other allied collections of tales assembled by Andrew Lang, including *The Animal Story Book* (1896), *The Arabian Nights Entertainments* (1898), *The Red Book of Animal Stories* (1899), *The Book of Romance* (1902), *The Red Romance Book* (1905), and *Tales of Greece and Troy* (1909).

Among his later illustrated works for other authors were M. R. James's *Old Testament Legends* (1913) and E. F. Benson's *David Blaize and the Blue Door* (1918), a delightful children's fantasy in the vein of *Alice's Adventures in Wonderland*.

In his late fifties he served as a private in the Artists' Rifles during the First World War.

Hospitalized in his final years, Henry J. Ford died in Repton on 19 November 1941. *The Times* obituary recalled: 'Those who knew him will remember his charming presence, and his enthusiasm for what he admired and enjoyed, which was very delightful.'

J. D. BATTEN

1860–1932

Very soon after the creation of the 'Fairy Book' partnership between Henry J. Ford and Andrew Lang, another successful collaboration was instigated by the London publisher David Nutt: J. D. Batten and Joseph Jacobs.

John Dixon Batten's imagination and style were very similar to those of Henry J. Ford. The two artists were exact contemporaries at the Slade, where both studied under, and were undoubtedly influenced by, the eminent painter and etcher Alphonse Legros. Joseph Jacobs was editor of the magazine *Folk Lore* and an eminent Jewish historian.

The first volume on which Batten and Jacobs collaborated was a definitive collection of fifty-three *English Fairy Tales* (1890). Many of these were the familiar classics – 'Jack and the Beanstalk', 'Tom Thumb', 'The Three Little Pigs' and 'The Three Bears' – but several hitherto unpublished folk tales, which had survived through the centuries by word of mouth only, were also printed here for the first time. In his preface, Jacobs praised 'the artistic skill with which my friend, Mr. J. D. Batten, has made the romance and humour of these stories live again in the brilliant designs with which he has adorned these pages.'

Batten and Jacobs next worked on *Celtic Fairy Tales* (1892), heroic and comic stories which introduced children to the unique magic of Celtic folk imagination from the Gaelic-speaking part of Scotland and the whole of Ireland. The success of these two collections led to *More English Fairy Tales* and *More Celtic Fairy Tales*, both published in 1894. The same team also collaborated on the equally charming and original *Indian Fairy Tales* (1892). The critic E. S. Hartland described these titles as 'the most delightful books of fairy tales, taking form and contents together, ever presented to children'.

J. D. BATTEN

In 1896 Jacobs and Batten produced *The Book of Wonder Voyages* which related the incredible journeys undertaken by the Argonauts, Maelduin, Hasan of Bessorah, Thorkill (to the Underworld) and Eric (to Paradise).

All these volumes were published by David Nutt, in both standard editions with very attractive cover designs by Batten, and large-paper copies printed on Japanese vellum.

One of the most important Christmas gift books for children in 1893 was *Fairy Tales from the Arabian Nights*, edited and arranged by E. Dixon, with five photogravure plates and many smaller illustrations, head- and tailpieces by J. D. Batten. The contents included eight of the best of Scheherazade's stories, together with all seven voyages of Sinbad the Sailor. *More Fairy Tales from the Arabian Nights*, including 'Aladdin', 'Ali Baba and the Forty Thieves' and 'The Fisherman and Genie', followed in 1894. A collected edition of these very popular books was published in 1907, and again revised in 1937.

Batten was later noted for his colour woodcuts in the Japanese style. He exhibited regularly at the Royal Academy (1891–1922) and was Secretary of the Society of Painters in Tempera for twenty years.

LOUIS RHEAD

1857–1926

Among the many artists of the era who illustrated the fairy tales of Hans Christian Andersen and the Brothers Grimm was the English-born Louis John Rhead, who emigrated to America and spent most of his artistic career in New York. Like his equally accomplished elder brother, George Woolliscroft Rhead, Louis was a versatile painter, etcher, ceramic designer and book illustrator. The brothers collaborated on editions of Bunyan's *The Pilgrim's Progress* and Tennyson's *Idylls of the King* (both 1898).

Louis Rhead's black and white drawings sometimes resemble the figurework of Henry J. Ford and Helen Stratton, but are not always as successful. He undertook many commissions for Harper (New York), illustrating the popular classics: Wyss's *Swiss Family Robinson* (1909), Hughes's *Tom Brown's School Days* (1911), Swift's *Gulliver's Travels* (1913), Andersen's *Fairy Tales and Wonder Stories* (1914), Stevenson's *Treasure Island* (1915), *Grimm's Fairy Tales* (1917), Lamb's *Tales from Shakespeare* (1918), Craik's *Fairy Book* (1922), and *Aesop's Fables* (1927).

HELEN STRATTON

Among the best of the folk lore collections to follow in the wake of Jacobs and Batten's *Celtic Fairy Tales* was Walter Douglas Campbell's *Beyond the Border* (1898), with 167 illustrations by Helen Stratton. Her imaginative art nouveau style often resembles that of J. D. Batten, especially in the decorative illustration of legends and fairy tales, princes and princesses, trolls and witches.

The peak of Helen Stratton's career was reached in 1899 with *The Fairy Tales of Hans Christian Andersen*, a handsome quarto art nouveau volume finely produced by George Newnes, with upwards of four hundred pen and ink illustrations. The artist's bold and humorous style was perfectly suited to the phantasmagorical world of 'The Little Mermaid', 'The Garden of Paradise', 'The Star Queen', 'The Emperor's New Clothes', and thirty other Andersen tales.

In the same year she collaborated with W. Heath Robinson (their styles were virtually identical at this time) and other artists to provide hundreds of illustrations for *The Arabian Nights Entertainments*, originally sold serially by Newnes in sixpenny parts, and then published as a large quarto. On both commissions, she must have been required to complete at least two or three illustrations each day to meet the tight deadlines.

Stratton's other books include Norman Gale's *Songs for Little People* in 1896 ('Miss Stratton has headed, tailed and bordered the verses with a series of exquisitely pictured fancies,' wrote the *Bookseller* critic), *Grimm's Fairy Tales* (1903), A. C. Herbertson's *Heroic Legends* (1908), Jean Lang's *A Book of Myths* (1915, with 16 colour plates), and George MacDonald's *The Princess and the Goblin* (1911) and *The Princess and Curdie* (1912). Her illustrations for the latter two classics were especially popular, and have been regularly reprinted.

52

H. R. MILLAR

1869–1942

'Nobody can illustrate tales of magic like H. R. Millar, whose enchanted castles, hairy savages and beautiful queens are beyond the pen and pencil of any other artist,' wrote J. B. Priestley in 1924 while reviewing the 11-volume new collected edition of E. Nesbit's *Children's Stories* (which contained Millar's illustrations). Then aged 30, Priestley came from the generation who were 'just old enough and young enough to have been children when the early stories were appearing as serials in the *Strand* magazine, and we can remember the fascination they exercised upon us month by month, and how we were entranced by Mr. H. R. Millar.'

Harold Robert Millar was born in Thornhill, Dumfriesshire, Scotland, and studied at the Birmingham Municipal School of Art. At the age of 22 he began working for the *Strand* magazine soon after its launch in 1891, and was soon recognized as their finest illustrator of children's stories. Beginning with Alexandre Dumas's 'The Enchanted Whistle' (May 1891) and Henry Sienkiewicz's 'Janko the Musician' (June 1891), Millar provided many hundreds of drawings for a large number of unfamiliar and newly translated folk tales and fairy stories (mainly European, by writers including Voltaire, Jokai, George Sand and Sarah Bernhardt). These were preserved for posterity in four handsome volumes – *The Golden Fairy Book* (1894), *The Silver Fairy Book* (1895), *The Diamond Fairy Book* (1897), and *The Ruby Fairy Book* (1898) – retaining all Millar's illustrations.

His legendary association with Edith Nesbit began in 1899 when he illustrated her magical tale, *The Seven Dragons* (reissued as *The Book of Dragons*, 1900). He continued to illustrate most of her wonderful stories in the *Strand*, and his delicate black and white drawings all survived in the books that followed

54

to captivate successive generations of children: *Nine Unlikely Tales for Children* (1901), *Five Children and It* (1902), *The Phoenix and the Carpet* (1904), *Oswald Bastable and Others* (1905, with H. M. Brock), *The Story of the Amulet* (1906), *The Enchanted Castle* (1907), *The House of Arden* (1908), *Harding's Luck* (1909), *The Magic City* (1910), *The Wonderful Garden* (1911), *The Magic World* (1912, with Spencer Pryse), and *Wet Magic* (1913), her last full-length children's book.

Millar's illustrations of the Phoenix, the Psammead, the Mouldiwarp, the Ugly-Wuglies, and all the other amazing denizens of Nesbit's magic worlds, are among the most loved and memorable in all children's literature. E. Nesbit's biographer, Doris Langley Moore, commented: 'There will be few ready to dispute H. R. Millar's pre-eminence as the interpreter of her invention. He fulfilled to something near perfection the exacting demands she made upon him.' Nesbit was convinced there must be a telepathic bond between herself and Millar, so perfect was his interpretation of her ideas and requirements.

Among the many other stories that Millar illustrated in the *Strand* were F. Anstey's *The Brass Bottle* (February–September 1900), Post Wheeler's *Stories for Children* (December 1911–September 1912) and several fairy tales by W. J. L. Kiehl (1913–17). He also worked non-stop for most of the other popular magazines of the period, including *Punch*, *Scraps*, *Fun*, *Little Folks*, *Chatterbox*, *Chums* and *The Girl's Own Paper*.

The dozens of children's books illustrated by Millar include *Fairy Tales Far and Near* retold by Q (Sir Arthur Quiller-Couch) (1895), Mrs Molesworth's *The Wood Pigeons and Mary* (1901) and *Peterkin* (1902), F. Anstey's *Only Toys!* (1903), Marie Corelli's *The Strange Visitation of Josiah McNason* (1904), Rudyard Kipling's *Puck of Pook's Hill* (1906) and *Rewards and Fairies* (1910), Tetta Ward's *My Fairy Tale Book* (1919), Robert Louis Stevenson's *The Merry Men* (1928) and *New Arabian Nights* (1928), Edith Walker's *Joyous Stories* (1935), A. S. K. Davis's *Isle of Adventure* (1937), and Geoffrey Mure's *The Boots and Josephine* (1939).

H. R. Millar's death in Surrey on 20 December 1942 went completely unnoticed by the press and his legions of admirers.

F. D. BEDFORD

1864–1954

Francis Donkin Bedford was born on 21 May 1864 in London, and studied at the Royal College of Art and Royal Academy Architectural School. He was articled to the noted architect Sir Arthur Blomfield before switching to painting and book illustration. His work was beautifully crafted and reflected his keen interest in design and architecture, although he was equally gifted in his portrayals of children and animals. By the turn of the century, his style and popularity rivalled that of H. R. Millar and Charles Robinson.

His early children's books include Jane Barlow's *The Battle of the Frogs and the Mice* (1894), S. Baring-Gould's *Old English Fairy Tales* (1895), *A Book of Nursery Rhymes* (1897), and his own *Night of Wonders* (1906).

In 1897 Bedford was invited by the writer E. V. Lucas to illustrate *A Book of Verses for Children*, and the great success of this volume encouraged Lucas to collaborate with Bedford on several more finely produced books: *The Book of Shops* (1899), *Four and Twenty Toilers* (1900), *The Visit to London* (1902), *Old-Fashioned Tales* (1905), *Forgotten Tales of Long Ago* (1906), *Another Book of Verses for Children* (1907), and *Runaways and Castaways* (1908).

Apart from these volumes, Bedford's most critically acclaimed illustrations accompanied Ann and Jane Taylor's *The 'Original Poems' and Others* (1903, centenary edition of this celebrated children's book) and the first book publication of J. M. Barrie's famous stage play, *Peter and Wendy* (1911). Bedford's later books include several by Charles Dickens (*The Magic Fishbone*, 1921; *A Christmas Carol*, 1923; *The Cricket on the Hearth*, 1927) and George MacDonald (*At the Back of the North Wind*, 1924; *The Princess and the Goblin*, 1926).

He died in May 1954, just after reaching his ninetieth birthday.

56

C. E. BROCK

1870–1938

Charles Edmund Brock was born in Holloway, north London, on 5 February 1870. The family settled in Cambridge, where his father was Reader in Oriental Languages at the University Press. He studied art under the sculptor Henry Wiles, and embarked on his prolific career as a book and magazine illustrator at the age of 21.

Two of his earliest children's books were Canon Atkinson's *Scenes in Fairyland* (1892) and Edwin Hartland's *English Fairy and Folk Tales* (1893). He became nationally known as an important new illustrator with two fine series of line drawings for Macmillan's Cranford volumes: *Humorous Poems of Thomas Hood* (1893, 130 illustrations) and *Gulliver's Travels* (1894, 100 illustrations). As was the custom of the time, these books carried extremely ornate and decorative pictures by the artist in gilt on the front covers. *Gulliver's Travels* shows Gulliver walking 'with the utmost circumspection', watched by hundreds of Lilliputians from an array of rooftops and Gothic towers, all in the richest gilt.

Charles E. Brock soon became established as a specialist in delicate Regency-style period illustration, in the tradition of Hugh Thomson. For over thirty years he was regularly asked to illustrate the favourite literary adult classics of the nineteenth century, by Jane Austen, Emily Brontë, Dickens, Gaskell, Irving, Kingsley, Lamb, Scott and Stevenson, together with more recent historical novels by Herbert Strang and Jeffery Farnol.

His children's books were relatively fewer, but the finest examples

C. E. BROCK

include E. Nesbit's *Oswald Bastable and Others* (1906, with H. R. Millar), *A Day Book for Girls* (1909), Eleanor Farjeon's *Martin Pippin in the Apple Orchard* (1921), *Children's Stories from Roumanian Legends* (1923), F. H. Burnett's *Little Lord Fauntleroy* (1925), Mrs Molesworth's *The Cuckoo Clock* (1931), and several editions of Charles Dickens' shorter pieces for the Christmas market (*The Chimes*, 1905; *The Cricket on the Hearth*, 1905; *A Christmas Carol*, 1905; *Dr Marigold*, 1908; *A Christmas Tree*, 1911).

Charles E. Brock died on 28 February 1938 at his Cambridge home.

H. M. BROCK

1875–1960

Henry Matthew Brock was born in Cambridge on 11 July 1875, and studied at the Cambridge School of Art. He shared a studio with his elder brother, Charles, where they stored a large collection of period costumes and furniture to be used in their period illustrations for exact accuracy. The artwork of the two brothers was very similar, though Henry concentrated more on action stories, including a vast number for boys' magazines (primarily for *The Captain*, and also the *Boy's Own Paper*) and annuals (*Blackie's* and *Herbert Strang's Annual*, *Oxford Annual for Boys*, among others).

"Readin' me a bit-by-the-week tale"

H. M. BROCK

We enjoyed ourselves awfully

Following the example of his brother, H. M. Brock illustrated many adult literary classics (even different editions of the same novels) by Jane Austen, Dickens, Gaskell, Kingsley, Scott, Stevenson, Thackeray, and Oliver Wendell Holmes. He also contributed prolifically to *Punch* from 1905 to 1940.

His most notable children's books are Mrs Ewing's *Jackanapes and Other Tales* (1913), John Lea's *Brave Boys and Girls in War Time* (1918), Eleanor Farjeon's *The Tale of Tom Tiddler* (1929), and Dickens' *Christmas Tales* (1932); but his most popular and enduring illustrations and colour plates proved to be the long-running series *The Fairy Library*, *The Old Fairy Tales*, *The Book of Fairy Tales*, and *The Book of Nursery Tales*, regularly reissued by Newnes and Warne in cheap formats and sets of individual titles (*Jack the Giant Killer*, *Valentine and Orson*, *Puss in Boots*, *Beauty and the Beast*, *Hop o'my Thumb*, etc.) and kept in print for successive generations of children to enjoy until quite recently. In 1915 the *Bookman* critic described Brock's *Old Fairy Tales* as 'masterpieces of modern art, with a picture on every page, besides several beautiful colour plates. Nobody could wish for more handsome picture-books at the amazingly low price.'

Among his later books are *The Bible Book of Golden Deeds* (1946), *The Children's Omnibus* (1947, including his illustrations for *Alice in Wonderland*), and *The Children's Pilgrim's Progress* (1950, fifty years after his original edition).

His final years were marred by failing eyesight; he died on 21 July 1960 in Cambridge.

"Explaining things to other bald-headed people."

HMBrock.

T. H. ROBINSON

1869–1950

Thomas Heath Robinson, born in Islington, north London, on 19 June 1869, was the eldest of three Robinson brothers, known collectively as 'The Three Musketeers', but ultimately not as successful or gifted as either Charles or William Heath Robinson. Tom was the third-generation namesake of 'Thomas Robinson' artists. Both his grandfather and father were proficient wood engravers.

After attending art school, Thomas Heath Robinson worked as assistant to his father. For thirty years, from 1895 to 1925, he was a very prolific book illustrator, beginning with Rinder's *Old-World Japan* (1895), Canton's *Child's Book of Saints* (1898) and Minssen's *Book of French Songs for the Young* (1899). In 1899 all three brothers collaborated on an edition of Hans Christian Andersen's *Fairy Tales*. Among his other book illustrations are Kingsley's *The Heroes* (1899), Creswick's *Robin Hood and his Adventures* (1902), Spenser's *Una and the Red Cross Knight* (1905), Oxenham's *Goblin Island* (1907), Wyss's *Swiss Family Robinson* (1913), Carroll's *Alice in Wonderland* (1922), and *The Child's Bible* (1928).

During the 1920s and 1930s he was kept extremely busy working for boys' magazines, especially *Chums*, for which he illustrated many of the popular adventure and public school stories. At this time he was the magazine's most important artist, the counterpart of H. M. Brock in *The Captain*. His drawings also decorated the pages of *Little Folks*, *Champion Annual*, *Holiday Annual*, and the *Herbert Strang's Annual*.

Unlike Charles and W. Heath, Thomas Robinson rarely attempted fantasy or imaginative art, usually concentrating on subjects requiring factual detail and historical accuracy.

CHARLES ROBINSON

1870–1937

The second of 'The Three Musketeers', Charles Robinson was born on 22 October 1870. Unlike his elder brother, he had a relatively sparse art education (mainly due to inadequate finances) and was essentially self-taught. While working with his brother at their father's studio, Charles attended evening classes and became devoted to the art of decoration and book design. His strongest influences in this field were William Morris and Walter Crane.

Robinson made a resounding impression with his first two books in 1895: a small edition of *Aesop's Fables* in Dent's Banbury Cross series, and his greatest success, the first illustrated edition of Robert Louis Stevenson's collection, *A Child's Garden of Verses*.

His graceful, sensitive, and often light-hearted portrayal of children, babies and fairies, surrounded by highly decorative borders and flowery chapter headings, became his trademark in the Golden Age, during which he illustrated and designed over a hundred books.

During the late 1890s he concentrated on black and white illustration, with Setoun's *The Child World* (1896), Coleridge's *Minstrel Dick* (1896), Field's *Lullaby Land* (1897), MacGregor's *King Longbeard* (1898), Bell's *The New Noah's Ark* (1899), and the magnificent three-volume *True Annals of Fairyland* (1900–2). After 1990 he also regularly used colour to great effect in *A Book of Days for Little Ones* (1901), *The Bairns Coronation Book* (1902), *Alice's Adventures in Wonderland* (1907), F. H. Burnett's *The Secret Garden* (1911), Shelley's *The Sensitive Plant* (1911), Perrault's *Fairy Tales* (1913), Wilde's *The Happy Prince* (1913), and 24 humorous Blackie books by W. Copeland.

Robinson himself also created his own characters in *The Ten Little Babies*

(1905), *Fanciful Fowls* (1906), *Peculiar Piggies* (1906) and *Black Bunnies* (1907), as well as the earlier *Christmas Dreams* (1896) which he wrote under the pseudonym 'Awfly Weirdly'.

Most of Robinson's illustrated works, especially the large Christmas gift books – *The Big Book of Fairy Tales* (1903), *The Big Book of Nursery Rhymes* (1911), and *The Big Book of Fables* (1912) – have very intricate and beautiful cover designs by the artist. Typical among Robinson's finely designed books of this period is H. Fielding-Hall's fairy story, *Margaret's Book* (1913), with 12 colour plates and 37 illustrations in the text as well as numerous decorative drawings. As a critic of the time remarked, 'It is a beautiful book to look at, illustrated with some of the most dainty and effective drawings that Mr. Charles Robinson – that prince among artists for children – has ever made, and produced with the utmost lavishness.'

The majority of his books for younger children were produced in a handy small format, with clear print ideal for the nursery and designed to induce children to want to handle and read the stories themselves.

In the closing years of the Golden Age, Robinson's output inevitably decreased, but his artwork remained as fresh and joyful as ever in *The Children's Garland of Verses* (1921), A. A. Milne's *Once On a Time* (1925), *Mother Goose Nursery Rhymes* (1928), *The Rubáiyát of Omar Khayyám* (1928), and *Granny's Book of Fairy Stories* (1930).

Busy and enthusiastic up to the end of his life, Charles Robinson died on 13 June 1937 while engaged on the construction of a model Spanish galleon. William Heath Robinson paid this tribute to his brother in *My Line of Life* in the following year: 'Charles was more concerned with his painting and his ship models than with theories about art. He was an artist first of all and last of all. He had the magic assistance so often given to genius.'

W. HEATH ROBINSON

1872–1944

William Heath Robinson, the youngest and subsequently the most famous of the 'Three Musketeer' brothers, was born on 31 May 1872 at Hornsey Rise, north London. He left school at the age of 15 to work in his father's studio, his only ambition being to follow the family tradition into the world of illustration.

His first sale was to the magazine *Little Folks*, but the earliest book commissions which came his way (from Bliss Sands) were not an auspicious start: the line drawings for *Danish Fairy Tales and Legends of Hans Andersen*, *Don Quixote*, and *The Pilgrim's Progress*, all in 1897, were crude and immature. More interesting were two collections of Indian fairy tales by W. H. D. Rouse: *The Giant Crab* (1897) and *The Talking Thrush* (1899).

In 1899 he collaborated with Helen Stratton and other artists to provide several hundred illustrations to *The Arabian Nights Entertainments*, originally sold serially in sixpenny parts, and then published as a large quarto. His drawings showed a strong influence of the art nouveau style, and are a distinct improvement on his earlier work in spite of the high speed of their execution (thirty drawings per month).

Heath Robinson's work as a gift book illustrator in the Edwardian decade ranged from the horrors of Poe and Rabelais to many children's classics. He joined Hodder & Stoughton at the same time as Edmund Dulac, and produced two of his finest series of watercolour plates for *Twelfth Night* (1908) and Kipling's *A Song of the English* (1909).

He then joined forces with Constable who published one of his most beautiful works, *Hans Andersen's Fairy Tales* (1913), with 16 colour plates and 93 line drawings. He was as ideally suited to the gentle and sentimental world of the

Little Mermaid and the Red Shoes, as Rackham had been to the grotesque and macabre world of the Brothers Grimm a few years earlier.

Following the practice of his brother Charles and many of the other great illustrators of the period, William Heath Robinson always designed the most striking and detailed covers for his gift books. *Hans Andersen's Fairy Tales* was bound in ornate red cloth with an ivory panel on the front, blocked in gilt with a design of storks and children.

Heath Robinson continued with Constable for three of his most happy productions. A *Midsummer Night's Dream* (1914) – in the artist's own words 'the most wonderful moonlight night in fantasy' – contained 12 colour plates with many line drawings and decorations, and a gilt cover design showing Titania, two fauns and a statue against a tree-lined background. Kingsley's *The Water Babies* (1915) and Walter de la Mare's *Peacock Pie* (1916) were equally delightful but less elaborate productions.

After the war, Heath Robinson's most important gift books for children were Charles Perrault's *Old Time Stories* (1921), Elsie Munro's *Topsy Turvy Tales* (1923): twelve humorous stories about lovers, ghosts and fairies, *Heath Robinson's Book of Goblins* (1934), and Dr Liliane Clopet's fairy stories, *Once Upon a Time* (1944), published shortly after the artist's death on 13 September 1944.

Two lesser-known titles, *The Child's Arabian Nights* (1903) and *Peter Quip in Search of a Friend* (1922), both written and illustrated by Heath Robinson, were issued with garish colour plates printed by chromolithography. Far better known today are his two greatest original fantasies, *The Adventures of Uncle Lubin* (1902) and *Bill the Minder* (1912), which both demonstrated the range and genius of his imagination perfectly, and have become classics of children's literature. Their success and great popularity with children of all ages (from 9 to 90) soon showed him where his true vocation lay: inventive humorous art rather than serious illustration.

Heath Robinson's agent A. E. Johnson wrote in a 1913 monograph of the artist:

I should portray Heath Robinson as a gentle amiable child, straying (with mouth and eyes open) through a world of commonplace wonders, admiringly observant of all about him – the odd shapes of trees, the whimsical cadence of the song of birds, the droll habits of perfectly respectable human persons – and vaguely conscious of a hidden significance in things which he does not attempt to probe . . .

Between the wars, at the same time that most contemporary illustrators were gradually retiring or fading from the scene due to the dearth of commissions, William Heath Robinson enjoyed a unique renaissance as the best-loved eccentric comic artist of the day, with a long run of books (*Absurdities*, *Let's Laugh*, *How to Live in a Flat*, *Railway Ribaldry*, etc.) featuring over-ingenious mechanical contrivances and ensuring the adjectival description 'Heath Robinson' a permanent place in the world's dictionaries.

'Heath Robinson lived in the age of science triumphant, when machinery had become a tyrant,' wrote Sir Kenneth Clark, 'and, as we all know, the man who ridicules tyrants is a champion of humanity.'

ARTHUR RACKHAM

1867–1939

Arthur Rackham, dubbed the 'Beloved Enchanter', was arguably the most successful and enduring artist in the Golden Age of children's book illustration. His name immediately evokes the image of a world of gnomes, fairies and dragons, gallant young knights and beautiful princesses – a direct inspiration for Walt Disney many years later. His watercolour paintings are memorable for their sepia tints and haunting backgrounds of twisted undergrowth and trees with sinister – often disturbing – personalities, menacing forests and gnarled woods. They cast a unique spell on adults and several generations of children (and they have been known to induce nightmares in more sensitive souls). To his friends and acquaintances, he is remembered as a gentle, loving and generous man, in appearance not unlike one of his own illustrations in *Grimm's Fairy Tales*.

Arthur Rackham was born in London on 19 September 1867. His talent for drawing, especially for fantastic subjects, showed itself at a very young age, when he smuggled pencil and paper to bed and drew on the pillows before going to sleep. At school his drawings, which included many humorous caricatures of the masters, were very successful and well received, and earned him the school prize.

From 1885 to 1892 Rackham worked as a clerk in the Westminster Fire Office, while attending art classes in the evenings and sending occasional sketches and contributions to illustrated magazines like *Scraps*, *Pall Mall Budget* and the *Daily Graphic*. He became a full-time professional artist at the age of 25 when he joined the staff of the newly formed *Westminster Budget*, caricaturing well-known politicians, actresses and members of the royal family.

Rackham's career as a book illustrator began modestly in 1893 but, unlike

Charles Brock and Charles Robinson (younger artists who were breaking into print at the same time), his early works were uninspired and indistinguishable from many other minor artists of the same period. Among these books were Adair-Fitzgerald's *The Zankiwank and the Bletherwick* (1896) and Browne's *Two Old Ladies* (1897). He also contributed drawings to *Chums*, *Little Folks*, and *Punch*, in more humorous vein.

The first important landmark in Rackham's career was *The Ingoldsby Legends* (Dent, 1898) with 102 illustrations which captured perfectly the humour of author Richard Barham. The critical success of this work resulted in three more commissions in quick succession: *Tales from Shakespeare* (1899), *Gulliver's Travels* (1900), and *Grimm's Fairy Tales* (1900, with 99 black and white illustrations and a colour frontispiece).

In 1903 Arthur Rackham married the gifted portrait painter Edyth Starkie, who proved to be his most stimulating and invaluable critic. The marriage coincided with the end of the workmanlike first stage of his career, and the beginning of Rackham's Golden Age. At the turn of the century, he was just one of a large number of very capable book illustrators. Five years later, he became recognized as a truly great artist, a genius without equal in his field.

The book that undoubtedly established Arthur Rackham as the leading decorative illustrator of the Edwardian era was his edition of *Rip Van Winkle*, published by William Heinemann in 1905. This large handsome volume, with 51 superb colour plates displaying the now familiar riverside and forest scenes, children and fairies, was the real launching pad of his creative and prolific career.

Simultaneous publication of a trade and de luxe edition – the latter was fully subscribed – and an exhibition of all the originals at the Leicester Galleries in London, set the pattern which was to be followed for over thirty years.

For many years, no Christmas was complete without a new sumptuous Rackham gift book. The inspired choice for 1906 was J. M. Barrie's *Peter Pan in*

Kensington Gardens, published by Hodder & Stoughton. The 50 colour plates were unanimously praised by all who saw them. One critic wrote: 'Mr. Rackham seems to have dropped out of some cloud in Mr. Barrie's fairyland, sent by special providence to make pictures in tune to his whimsical genius.' An enlarged version was published in 1912 with a new colour frontispiece and seven additional full-page black and white illustrations. The *Peter Pan Portfolio* appeared that same year.

Rackham's edition of *Alice's Adventures in Wonderland* was the most popular of the seven which appeared in 1907, following the expiry of the British copyright. Although there was some heated criticism, mainly from admirers of the original Alice illustrator, John Tenniel (then still alive at 87), several critics found Rackham's Alice much more acceptable and charming than Tenniel's 'stiff wooden puppet'.

The majority of Rackham's books from 1907 (*Alice*) to 1926 (*The Tempest*) were published by William Heinemann, with only two lesser works issued by Hodder & Stoughton in 1921 and 1922. *Alice* was soon followed by the revised 'definitive' edition of *The Ingoldsby Legends* (1907) with redrawn and recoloured illustrations. Rackham's three books from 1899 to 1900 – *Tales from Shakespeare, Gulliver's Travels*, and *Grimm's Fairy Tales* – were similarly enlarged and recoloured, all in 1909, with opulent de luxe editions to match. *A Midsummer Night's Dream* (1908) is another of Rackham's much-loved creations, with the delightful images of the fairies, Puck, Titania and Bottom, Helena and Hermia. His contract with Heinemann for this book meant that he had to turn down

ARTHUR RACKHAM

Methuen's request to illustrate Kenneth Grahame's *The Wind in the Willows*, a book very dear to his heart. That commission had to wait for thirty years.

Rackham was now internationally famous, and his paintings were exhibited in most of the European capitals, where they were acquired for the leading galleries of Paris, Vienna, and other cities.

After the German classics, *Undine* (1909), *The Rhinegold and the Valkyrie* (1910) and *Siegfried and the Twilight of the Gods* (1911), came *Aesop's Fables* (1912) and *Mother Goose–The Old Nursery Rhymes* (1913). The Aesop illustrations contain several self-caricatures of Rackham, including the man who catches the flea; and a drawing of the artist's home in Chalcot Gardens (north London) appears as the House that Jack Built in *Mother Goose*.

Arthur Rackham's Book of Pictures (1913) includes the complete range of all his styles and moods: 44 colour plates of the little people, fairy tales, children, grotesque and fantastic, classic and 'various' themes. Among the splendid illustrations in this book are 'Cupid's Alley' (acquired by the Tate Gallery), and the monstrous 'Leviathan' and 'Fog'. In the latter, the supplicating couple under the fog monster are Rackham and his wife!

Following the outbreak of war in 1914, Rackham went into uniform with the Hampstead Volunteers and helped the war effort by digging trenches in Essex, while still finding time to complete his annual gift book commissions: *A Christmas Carol* (1915), *The Allies' Fairy Book* (1916), Malory's *The Romance of King Arthur* (1917), Grimm's *Little Brother and Little Sister* (1917), *English Fairy Tales Retold* (1918), *Some British Ballads* (1919), *Cinderella* (1919), *The Sleeping Beauty* (1920), and *Irish Fairy Tales* (1920). In spite of the decline in the gift books' production values after the war, Rackham continued to be the busiest illustrator of the period.

The popularity of Arthur Rackham's books was as great, if not greater, in the United States as it was in Britain, and there were many successful exhibitions of his work at New York art galleries. He was inundated by letters from admirers from all over the world (and he tried to answer every one), including the most

78

remote parts of the American continent where his fans regularly ordered his books. He did not visit the US until 1927, and was amazed to be feted as a celebrity everywhere he went.

After 1920 he accepted several requests to illustrate American classics: Nathaniel Hawthorne's *A Wonder Book* (1922), Christopher Morley's *Where the Blue Begins* (1925), Washington Irving's *The Legend of Sleepy Hollow* (1928), and Edgar Allan Poe's *Tales of Mystery and Imagination* (1935). These were all as powerful as his earlier work, though he was unable to equal Harry Clarke's unique imagery for Poe.

George Harrap became Rackham's most regular publisher after 1925 (following Harry Clarke's departure from his company), and among the most popular titles from this period are *The Tempest* (1926), *The Vicar of Wakefield* (1929), *The Compleat Angler* (1931), and *The Arthur Rackham Fairy Book* (1933). His favourite undertaking for Harrap was the edition of Hans Andersen's *Fairy Tales* (1932). Rackham visited Denmark in 1931 with his daughter Barbara to absorb the atmosphere, visit farms and local museums, and make copious notes and sketches. In Copenhagen he met an old lady who had heard Andersen himself reading some newly written stories over seventy years before.

The brilliant swan song of Rackham's career resulted from a meeting with the American, George Macy, in 1936. Macy gave Rackham two years and a contract to illustrate *The Wind in the Willows* for the Limited Editions Club of New York. All the artist's wisdom, happiness and affectionate humour shines through the 16 illustrations, the last of which was completed shortly before his death on 6 September 1939, two weeks before his seventy-second birthday. Bruce Rogers, one of the greatest American book designers, prepared and signed the volume for the Limited Editions Club in 1940. The first English edition did not appear until ten years later, and this was followed in 1951 by the de luxe 'Hundredth Edition' of the book.

EDMUND DULAC

1882–1953

If Arthur Rackham was considered to be the most universally popular (and constantly reprinted) artist in the Golden Age of children's book illustration, Edmund Dulac ranked a close second, and many connoisseurs judged him to be the greater of the two. Dulac's expressive use of colour, hitherto unprecedented in British book illustration, combined with a passionate interest in Persian and Indian miniatures, evoked all the mystery and exoticism of the East. Describing Dulac's colour plates, one critic observed that 'each of these little irridescent miniatures which seem to be made of opal dust on mother of pearl, satisfies the demand which Delacroix made upon all paintings – they are colour feasts for the eye.'

ARTHUR RACKHAM

plate 18

ARTHUR RACKHAM

plate 19

ARTHUR RACKHAM

plate 20

W. HEATH ROBINSON

plate 21

W. HEATH ROBINSON

plate 22

EDMUND DULAC

plate 23

EDMUND DULAC

plate 24

WILLY POGANY

plate 25

HARRY CLARKE

plate 26

KAY NIELSEN

plate 27

KAY NIELSEN

plate 28

WARWICK GOBLE

plate 29

WILLIAM M. TIMLIN

plate 30

E. J. DETMOLD

plate 31

E. J. DETMOLD

plate 32

RENÉ BULL

plate 33

EDMUND DULAC

Edmund Dulac was born in Toulouse, France, on 22 October 1882, the son of a commercial traveller. He began drawing and painting at a very early age, and his holidays were spent copying Japanese prints. After two boring years studying law at university, he attended full-time art classes at the École des Beaux Arts. Inspired by the work of the great English artists, and the book illustrations of Walter Crane and William Morris, he soon became an ardent Anglophile.

In 1903 he won a scholarship to the Académie Julien in Paris, under the esteemed Jean-Paul Laurens, who was to be the tutor of Kay Nielsen at the same art school only four years later. However, Dulac soon became disillusioned and unhappy with both the school and the city, and returned home to Toulouse after only three weeks.

He decided to concentrate on magazine illustration, and, as England was the most lucrative field for such work, London was the natural mecca of his dreams. Armed with a large portfolio of drawings and a list of important London publishers, he settled there permanently in the autumn of 1904.

Dulac was only 22 when his first commission came from J. M. Dent to illustrate a new edition of the complete novels of the Brontë sisters. Several more commissions from magazines also kept him busy, and one of the earliest children's stories he illustrated was Mrs Molesworth's 'Cruel Kindness' (*Pall Mall*, January 1906). His work blossomed in this medium, becoming innovative and mature.

The first children's book to be illustrated by Dulac was Mrs Stawell's *Fairies I Have Met* (1907; later reissued as *My Days with the Fairies*), published with a delightful cover design and eight colour plates in a style very close to Rackham.

During the same year, Arthur Rackham left Hodder & Stoughton for Heinemann, and Dulac immediately filled his place with a sumptuous edition of *Stories from the Arabian Nights*, published in November 1907 for the Christmas market. Following the Hodder style and presentation of Rackham's *Peter Pan* the previous year, Dulac's 50 mounted colour plates were set together as a group at the end of the volume (a practice soon abandoned in later editions). The artist's mock-Persian lettering on the cover harmonized perfectly with the exotic feel of the tales.

As opposed to Rackham, who usually preferred to tint his pen and ink originals with a minimum of colour, Dulac remained true to the medium of watercolour, and the critics were unanimous in their praise. He was recognized as an illustrator of the first rank, a master of the fantastic and exotic, and 'a dreamer of extraordinary dreams'.

The *Arabian Nights* was the first of ten ornate gift books illustrated by Dulac during the ensuing decade. It always remained his most popular work and was reprinted several times in cheaper formats with reduced numbers of plates.

Dulac's edition of *The Tempest* was published in November 1908, simultaneously with Rackham's edition of Shakespeare's other classic comedy, *A Midsummer Night's Dream*. He created a Rackham-like world on Prospero's island, inhabited by elves, goblins, and a benevolent Caliban. Outstanding among these watercolours was the one entitled 'We are such stuff as dreams are made on', showing the creation of the universe from primeval chaos.

An entirely different enterprise was assembled and published by Frederick Warne in November 1908, at the same time as *The Tempest*. This was the delightful collection *Lyrics Pathetic and Humorous from A to Z*, a children's alphabet in the form of elaborate limericks created by Dulac two years earlier, with 24 colour plates. These illustrations demonstrated to the public for the first time Dulac's genius for caricature, a genre he would explore fully over the next forty years.

The obvious choice for Dulac's 1909 Christmas gift book was *The Rubáiyát of Omar Khayyám*, as that year marked the centenary of the birth of Edward Fitzgerald, the poem's best-known translator. The 20 superb colour plates again show Dulac at his most imaginative, revelling in this cornucopia of Eastern fantasy.

The Sleeping Beauty, and Other Fairy Tales (1910) was a selection of stories by Perrault and Grimm, retold by Sir Arthur Quiller-Couch. Dulac designed a beautiful cover for the de luxe edition, decorated in gold embossed on rich brown morocco, depicting an assortment of gilt cherubs sitting on Bluebeard's scimitar, Cinderella's glass slipper, and other key symbols from the tales. Dulac's close friend Elsa Bignardi served as model for the Sleeping Beauty and Bluebeard's wife; she married Dulac in the following spring.

Dulac's 1911 gift book was *Stories from Hans Andersen*. Among the 28 colour plates in this volume are several of the artist's most loved and celebrated illustrations: 'The Little Mermaid', 'The Emperor's New Clothes' and 'The Princess and the Pea'. Some of the stories, including 'The Wind's Tale' and 'The Snow Queen', were later reissued with Dulac plates in separate smaller volumes.

Now in his thirtieth year, Dulac was a much feted, prominent and debonair figure in the London social scene, and the country's favourite 'Anglo-Frenchman'. In February 1912 he became a fully naturalized British citizen.

After a venture into the macabre world of *The Bells, and Other Poems* (1912) by Edgar Allan Poe, Dulac returned to more 'Arabian Nights' with *Princess Badoura* (1913) and *Sinbad the Sailor* (1914).

Following the outbreak of the First World War, Hodder & Stoughton asked Dulac to prepare a compilation of his own favourite artwork. Published at the intentionally low price of three shillings to guarantee huge sales, *Edmund Dulac's Picture-Book for the French Red Cross* made an outright profit of £1,000 for that organization, an invaluable amount which undoubtedly helped to save many lives in those dark and tragic months. The book contained 20 colour plates, mainly taken from Dulac's previous book and magazine illustrations, together with a splendid new watercolour for 'The Story of the Bird Feng'.

Every drawing produced by Dulac in 1915 was done without personal salary, all profits going to war charities. These included his colour plates for two fairy story books by Queen Marie of Roumania, *The Dreamer of Dreams* (1915) and *The Stealers of Light* (1916).

The critic Martin Birnbaum wrote that the 15 colour plates in *Edmund Dulac's Fairy Book – Fairy Tales of the Allied Nations* (1916) represented

a unique commentary on the artist's resourcefulness and wonderful power of assimilation. In each painting he magically develops what appears superficially to be a new style, peculiarly appropriate to the nationality of the particular story, but ever remaining

Dulac's own. Surely no other artist has, within the limits of a single volume, exhausted not only the hues of the rainbow, but so many regions of the earth. Japan's rhythm and refinement, Servia's barbaric patterns, the white snows and passionate ringing colours of Russia, French grace, languorous Italian beauty, Belgian quaintness, and wholesome English charm are all to be found here.

Dulac's last gift book for Hodder & Stoughton was Nathaniel Hawthorne's *Tanglewood Tales* (1918). Of the 14 colour plates, 'Minotaur' and 'Europa and the Bull' were singled out for special praise.

His 10 colour plates for Leonard Rosenthal's *The Kingdom of the Pearl* (1920) all depict scenes from Persian and Indian mythology.

After the end of the war in 1918, Dulac turned to many other pursuits including art psychology, interior decoration, horoscopes, making bamboo flutes and compiling monthly crosswords for the *Pall Mall* magazine.

Although Rackham was kept continuously busy during the inter-war years with gift book illustrations, only two similar commissions came to Dulac in the late 1920s. Stevenson's *Treasure Island* was published by Ernest Benn in 1927, with 12 colour plates and several drawings and decorations throughout the text. Dulac's illustrations here are soft and dreamlike, in composition quite unlike the strong colours of his Hodder classics. They were among the artist's own favourites.

His last important children's book was *A Fairy Garland, being Fairy Tales from the Old French* (1928) selected by the artist himself, with 12 colour plates.

During the last fifteen years of his life, Edmund Dulac gained a permanent worldwide audience for his artwork as a pioneer designer of postage stamps and banknotes. His first design was the brown 1½d Coronation stamp (12 May 1937) with a joint portrait of King George VI and Queen Elizabeth. Five hundred million were printed. Many more followed: the King's cameo portrait on the definitive issues from 1937 onwards, and complete designs on all values over 6d; the Olympic Games winged victory stamp (1948); the Festival of Britain (1951); the definitive Elizabeth II issues in 1952; and the 1s 3d Coronation stamp in 1953.

By the early 1940s, Dulac was an acknowledged master of this artform, and it was no surprise when General de Gaulle personally chose the celebrated Anglo-Frenchman to design all the banknotes and postage stamps of 'France Libre' which carried the unifying symbol of the Cross of Lorraine. This extended to all the French colonies (the stamps of Cameroun, Guadeloupe, Martinique, West Africa, etc.) linked with the exiled French Government in their fight against Germany. The definitive 'Marianne' stamp of 1944 is signed 'Edmond Dulac' in the lower right corner, using the French form of his Christian name. After the war, Dulac designed the banknotes of Spain, Italy, Turkey and several other countries.

With no more work forthcoming from British book publishers after the war, Dulac signed a contract with the Limited Editions Club of New York for a series of classics to be selected by the artist himself. Only three were completed and published: Pushkin's *The Golden Cockerel* (1950), Pater's *The Marriage of Cupid and Psyche* (1951) and Milton's *Masque of Comus* (1954).

Edmund Dulac died on 25 May 1953, only a few days before the release of his Coronation stamp.

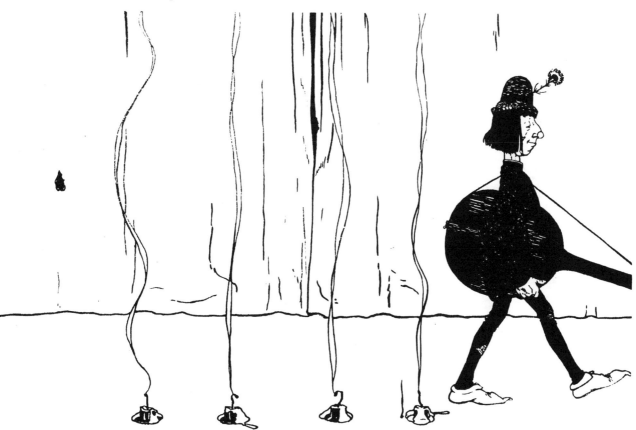

WILLY POGANY

1882–1955

Willy Pogany was Dulac's most successful European contemporary during the highest peak of the Golden Age of book illustration in London between 1906 and 1915. Like his friend Dulac (who was only two months younger than Pogany), he graduated to London via early training in Paris, and was similarly influenced by Chinese and Japanese art and illuminated manuscripts.

Born in Szeged, Hungary, on 24 August 1882, William Andrew Pogany studied at Budapest Technical University, and at art schools in Munich and Paris before moving to London at the age of 23.

His first illustrated children's books to appear in London (all in 1907) were W. Jenkyn Thomas's *The Welsh Fairy Book*, Mary Ward's *Milly and Olly*, and G. E. Farrow's *Adventures of a Dodo*. He also fulfilled commissions for many other popular new books including Gerald Young's *The Witch's Garden* and H. de Vere Stacpoole's *The Blue Lagoon*.

Pogany was best known for his series of sumptuous annual gift books for George Harrap, beginning with *A Treasury of Verse for Little Children* (1908) and *The Rubáiyát of Omar Khayyám* (1909). For the adult market he illustrated *The Rime of the Ancient Mariner* (1910) and the Wagner trilogy *Tannhäuser* (1911), *Parsifal* (1912) and *Lohengrin* (1913). *The Rime of the Ancient Mariner* was his most ornate and impressive production, with hand-scripted text, full-page black and white drawings and colour plates tipped-in on grey matte paper. This combination of illustration and calligraphic text by the artist was rarely repeated. (Timlin's *The Ship that Sailed to Mars*, also published by Harrap, was the only post-war gift book to be issued in the same format.) In 1913 Pogany illustrated Heine's *Atta Troll*, *The Hungarian Fairy Book* (reflecting his keen

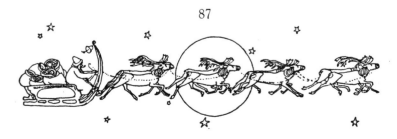

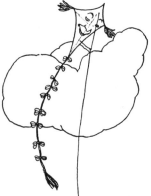

interest in his native country's peasant art), and *Forty-Four Turkish Fairy Tales*.

In 1914 Pogany created and designed two new series of fairy tale books in the hallowed tradition of Crane and Caldecott, each published at one shilling per volume to attract a wide audience. The 'Willy Pogany Children' set (*Hiawatha*; *The Three Bears*; *Red Riding Hood*; *Robinson Crusoe*; and *The Children at the North Pole*) each comprised 14 coloured 6 in × 5 in plates printed alongside in a single folding strip measuring 70 inches long when fully extended, with accompanying letterpress on the verso.

His other bestselling shilling picture books for small children were published in the following year (July 1915): *The Gingerbread Man*; *Cinderella*; *Little Mother Goose* (containing all the favourite nursery rhymes like 'Little Jack Horner', 'Old King Cole', and 'Miss Muffet') and *The Children of Japan*, a story in rhyme by Grace Bartruse, retailing Jack and Jill's visit to an idyllic Japan.

Unlike Dulac, Pogany was not a naturalized British citizen, and soon after the outbreak of war emigrated with his family to America where he took up permanent residence.

He continued to illustrate many more children's books including *Alice's Adventures in Wonderland* (1929), *My Poetry Book* (1934), and Padraic Colum's collection of Irish folk tales *The Frenzied Prince* (1943), but none of these approached the Harrap production values, and his colour plates often appeared garish.

Pogany designed scenery and costumes for the New York Metropolitan Opera House, mural decorations for William Randolph Hearst and many public buildings and galleries, and lived in Hollywood for a time working on films and painting portraits of the stars, before settling in New York. He died on 30 July 1955.

KAY NIELSEN

1886–1957

Kay Nielsen was a brilliant colourist and a highly decorative illustrator, able to introduce images that were sometimes strikingly fantastic or bizarre. All his life he had an affinity for the Oriental, and his works come nearest in quality to Middle Eastern or Persian designs. He was also a specialist in elaborate rococo motifs and stippling effects which are reminiscent of Aubrey Beardsley.

This celebrated Danish artist was born in Copenhagen on 12 March 1886. His father was the Director of the Royal Danish Theatre, and his mother, Oda Larssen, was a very popular singer and actress. Henrik Ibsen and Jonas Lie were among the famous writers who visited the Nielsen household, and the young Kay was inspired to illustrate the traditional Norse sagas as they were read aloud by his mother.

He studied art in Paris from 1904 to 1911 at Colarossi's and the Académie Julien (where Edmund Dulac was a pupil five years earlier). A tall, stooping figure, addicted to cigarettes, Nielsen was remembered by his comrades in the Latin Quarter as being invariably courteous and friendly, much loved and admired by everyone he knew.

His most productive period began in 1911, after he moved to London. At his first exhibitions all the critics realized that Nielsen's artistic talents were quite original and of a very unusual kind. The incisive line was uniquely his own, and his depictions of fairyland less sombre than Rackham's. This critical success led to his first commission from Hodder and Stoughton, who were to publish all of Kay Nielsen's greatest productions. The first book was entitled *In Powder and Crinoline* (1913), a collection of lesser-known old fairy tales retold by Sir Arthur Quiller-Couch. The idea for this sumptuous volume was originally Nielsen's, and his 24 colour illustrations (including an oval frontispiece, plus many decorations) ranged in style from delicate to the disturbingly menacing.

By general consent, Nielsen's most spectacular and celebrated book is *East of the Sun and West of the Moon*, old tales from the North, translated from the Norwegian of Peter C. Asbjornsen and Jorgen Moë (devoted collectors of Scandinavian folk lore in the mid-nineteenth century). First published in 1914, this beautiful volume has been reprinted many times up to the present day. Martin Birnbaum, one of Nielsen's earliest admirers, wrote of this book:

His most intricate inventions never seem laboured. Controlled in a measure by Norse ornamental traditions, he reaches an absolute equality with the poetical text, and it is a genuine pleasure to reach the oasis of a Kay Nielsen picture in a journey through the printed pages of a book . . . He has mounted so freely and easily into a realm entirely his own that we can enthusiastically join the London and continental throngs which have long since surrendered to the intensity of conviction which we feel in these works.

Nielsen's unique style and talent for combining the eerie and fantastic with beautiful decorative effect was at its peak with this set of illustrations.

Drawing in pen and ink, enhanced by watercolour, with an immaculate technique, Nielsen's beautiful books were always embellished with his designs for endpapers, frieze-like patterns, initial letters, and other decorative motifs.

After the First World War, Nielsen was the chief stage designer at the Danish State Theatre until 1923. His imagination was allowed full sway with exotic scenes of the most fantastic splendour and beauty in a series of spectacular theatrical epics, among them *Scaramouche* and *Aladdin* (a performance so lengthy it extended over two evenings). During the same period, he painted a series of illustrations for *The Rubáiyát of Omar Khayyám*, and *A Thousand and One Nights*. Plans to reproduce the latter in book form were aborted owing to the very high costs of quality printing after the war.

Nielsen returned to London in 1924 when Hodder & Stoughton published his edition of *Hans Andersen's Fairy Tales*. He followed this a year later with a companion volume of tales by the Brothers Grimm, *Hansel and Gretel, and Other*

Stories. In 1930 Nielsen illustrated *Red Magic*, a collection of the world's best fairy tales, edited and arranged by Romer Wilson.

In 1936 Nielsen made his first trip to California with his wife, and decided to settle in Los Angeles two years later. Living on the periphery of Hollywood and the film world, he was occasionally employed as a set designer on movies, among them *Fantasia*. This work soon dried up, and his reputation was quickly forgotten with the advent of war. At the age of 55, he was forced to earn money as a chicken farmer, living with his wife in a small mortgaged cottage outside Los Angeles.

Salvation came in 1942 with a commission to paint a large mural called 'The First Spring' for a multi-racial high school. The finished work measured 34 feet long by 19 feet high, and was described by one leading art critic as being 'one of the most beautiful wall paintings in America'. One year after this unique work of art was completed, the school was closed down and taken over by the Board of Education's business offices. Nielsen's mural was stripped from the wall, and replaced with charts of urban school districts!

A later, more durable, commission was an altar painting based on the 23rd Psalm for the Wong Chapel in the First Congregational Church of Los Angeles. This was completed in 1947, after which there was no more work for another six years. Even in his native Denmark, to which he and his wife Ulla returned briefly in desperation, Nielsen's art was no longer wanted. The couple remained in artistic obscurity until Nielsen's death in June 1957 at the age of 71. His funeral took place at the same church in Los Angeles where his painting of the 23rd Psalm hung over the altar of the Wong Chapel.

WARWICK GOBLE

1862–1943

Warwick Goble was one of the busiest and most versatile British illustrators of the Golden Age, at home with any subject that came his way, from a battle scene to a tea party. He gradually developed into a notable specialist of Japanese and Indian subjects, with a distinctive style recalling both Edmund Dulac and René Bull.

He was born on 22 November 1862 in Dalston, north London, the son of a commercial traveller, and studied at the City of London School, where he displayed an early talent for watercolour painting.

During the 1890s he was in great demand with commissions from the growing numbers of popular monthly magazines, and contributed innumerable half-tone illustrations to *Little Folks*, *Strand*, *Pearsons*, *Wide World*, *The Boy's Own Paper*, and many others.

Early science fiction, and the 'weirdly imaginative', became his particular forte towards the end of the century; and his major contribution to the genre was a superb set of 66 illustrations which accompanied the first appearance in print of *The War of the Worlds* (*Pearsons* magazine, April–December 1897) by H. G. Wells. A selection of Goble's plates were reproduced in the American first edition of 1898.

Goble enjoyed travelling, and roamed the world in search of local colour, always preferring solitude to society. In his lone occupations of cycling and boating, sketching and smoking, his acquaintances said 'he would be happy if he were on speaking terms with no one in the world'.

He kept busy illustrating several popular editions of children's books, including R. M. Ballantyne's *Young Fur Traders*, Mrs Molesworth's *The Grim*

House (1899), Gordon Stables's *Young Peggy McQueen* (1903), and F. Whishaw's *The Emperor's Englishman* (1896).

Goble moved into the big time in 1909 when he became the resident gift book illustrator for the large publishing firm of Macmillan. The first of his classic de luxe volumes in the Macmillan series was *The Water Babies*, by Charles Kingsley. Containing 32 fine mounted colour plates by Goble, this ranks as one of the most beautiful editions ever published of this delightful classic. His second de luxe volume was the equally stunning *Green Willow, and Other Japanese Fairy Tales* (1910) by Grace James. In these 40 colour illustrations, Goble was allowed free rein with his first love, proving that he was second to none in his portrayal of Oriental subjects. This was followed in quick succession by Basile's *Stories from the Pentamerone* (1911), Lal Behari Day's *Folk-Tales of Bengal* (1912), and Mrs D. M. Craik's *The Fairy Book* (1913).

During the First World War, Goble was employed in the drawing office at Woolwich Arsenal, and also gave voluntary service to the British Red Cross in France. The last of his sumptuous gift books was published two years after the war: *The Book of Fairy Poetry* (1920), edited by Dora Owen.

After occasional artwork for the New York firm of Macmillan, including an edition of Stevenson's *Treasure Island* in 1923, Warwick Goble gradually gave up professional illustrating, and concentrated on his recreations of sculling, cycling and travel. He died at his Surrey home on 22 January 1943, a few weeks after his eightieth birthday.

RENÉ BULL

1872–1942

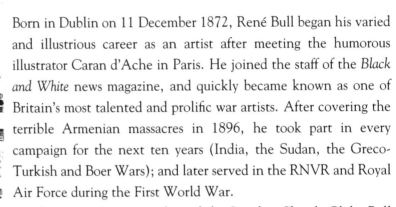

Born in Dublin on 11 December 1872, René Bull began his varied and illustrious career as an artist after meeting the humorous illustrator Caran d'Ache in Paris. He joined the staff of the *Black and White* news magazine, and quickly became known as one of Britain's most talented and prolific war artists. After covering the terrible Armenian massacres in 1896, he took part in every campaign for the next ten years (India, the Sudan, the Greco-Turkish and Boer Wars); and later served in the RNVR and Royal Air Force during the First World War.

As a prominent member of the London Sketch Club, Bull was a close friend and associate of fellow members Cecil Aldin, John Hassall, Phil May and Edmund Dulac. His Edwardian book illustrations included Jean de la Fontaine's *Fables* (1905) and Joel Chandler Harris's *Uncle Remus* (1906).

Like Dulac and Goble, René Bull was greatly influenced by Oriental art. His travels to the Middle East provided expert knowledge of Arab customs and costume, which led to his greatest and most admired book illustrations, *The Arabian Nights* (1912) and *The Rubáiyát of Omar Khayyám* (1913). The latter was acclaimed by the *Bookman* critic:

In his unmistakably individual manner, Mr. René Bull has caught in these remarkable paintings the spirit and atmosphere of Fitzgerald's immortal adaptation: the glowing imagination, the sombre occultism, the mystery and Oriental magnificence of the poem are sensitively and glamorously expressed in his beautiful, ornately decorative work.

After the war
he illustrated Hans Andersen's
Fairy Tales and Scott's *Gulliver's Travels*.

At home in London he became a devoted model enthusiast, and was responsible for the working model of the Zeebrugge raid at the British Empire Exhibition (1924–5).

René Bull died on 14 March 1942.

EDWARD J. DETMOLD

1883–1957

The Detmold twins were a unique phenomenon in British art, recognized by their contemporaries as a single creative personality 'divided between two bodies'. Their remarkable etchings and watercolours of plants and animals, minutely detailed in the Japanese manner, are all prized collector's items.

Charles Frederick and Edward Barton Detmold were born in Putney, south London, on 21 November 1883. Their middle names were later replaced by 'Maurice' and 'Julius', but the two boys were generally called Maurice and Edward, their published work appearing jointly as 'M. & E. Detmold'.

At the age of 5 the twins developed a dual passion for drawing and observing animals, and made regular sketching expeditions to Regent's Park Zoo and the Natural History Museum in South Kensington, where they drew detailed sketches of shells, crayfish, monkey skulls, and hundreds of other animal subjects.

Their first book, *Pictures from Birdland*, comprising 24 colour plates, was published by J. M. Dent for the Christmas market in 1899. The Detmolds' most celebrated joint achievement, and among the finest book illustrations ever produced, was the set of 16 watercolours depicting scenes from Rudyard Kipling's *The Jungle Book*. Macmillan first issued these in November 1903, contained in a green linen portfolio (at the de luxe price of five guineas per set); and in book form, with the plates much reduced, five years later. These paintings were praised for their realistic detail and decorative arrangement. Together with the plates of Mowgli and Baloo, Maurice's depiction of Kaa the Python is especially powerful.

Maurice suddenly committed suicide in April 1908. Edward was devastated, feeling that half of his own soul and personality had died with his brother.

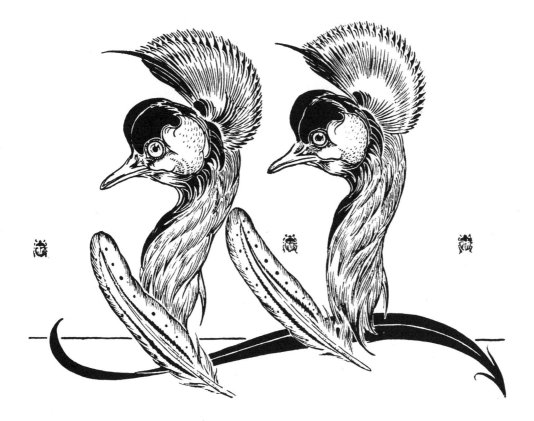

Nevertheless he was determined to carry on with all the various ideas and projects they had originally planned in unison.

He joined the ranks of Hodder & Stoughton's immortal band of gift book illustrators (alongside Edmund Dulac and W. Heath Robinson) with the superb 1909 edition of *Aesop's Fables*. His 25 colour plates of the Vain Jackdaw, the Eagle and his Captor, the She-Goats and their Beards, and all the other fabular animals, were perfectly suited to the artist's talents. His decorated cover was pictorially gilt-stamped with a design showing one of Detmold's favourite motifs, a large bird with wings outstretched.

He was then commissioned by the *Illustrated London News* to prepare a series for Kipling's *The Second Jungle Book*, and these were published in seven issues of this periodical from October 1910 to January 1911, but (unlike the 1903 set of paintings) were never issued in book form.

For George Allen, Detmold illustrated Lemonnier's *Birds and Beasts* (1911), and two de luxe volumes by the Nobel prizewinner Maurice Maeterlinck, *The Life of the Bee* (1911) and *Hours of Gladness* (1912).

He returned to Hodder & Stoughton with another popular animal series for children: *The Book of Baby Birds* (1912), *The Book of Baby Pets* (1913), *The Book of Baby Dogs* (1914), and *Our Little Neighbours* (1921).

His final two opulent gift books for Hodder & Stoughton were *Fabre's Book of Insects* (1921), with 12 remarkable colour studies of the beautiful and bizarre denizens of the insect world as seen through Detmold's 'microscope' eye; and *The Arabian Nights* (1924), a very successful change of direction into the realms of exotic fantasy.

On the strength of *The Arabian Nights*, Detmold could have become one of the greatest illustrators of fantasy and fairy stories. He took great care and much time to complete a set of colour plates for Hans Andersen's *Fairy Tales*; but Hodder's schedules and backlists were already full with editions of these stories, since they had already published Edmund Dulac, Heath Robinson and Kay Nielsen in turn, and they could not use Detmold's Andersen illustrations (unpublished to this day).

During the 1920s Detmold continued to draw, paint, and hold exhibitions of etchings and drypoints, but it was not long before he retired completely from public life. As a manic depressive and sensitive soul who could not abide the violence and disorder in society, he lived as a complete recluse with his widowed sister in a remote part of Montgomeryshire. On 1 July 1957 he committed suicide, nearly half a century after the death of his twin brother.

The art critic and family friend Campbell Dodgson recorded his impressions of the twins as follows:

I do not remember in the history of art another case in which twin brothers, sharing an equal talent, lived and worked together in close companionship as two young English-men, Charles Maurice and Edward Julius Detmold, did till a few years ago. They seemed as one soul divided between two bodies, possessing the same quickness of eye and deftness of hand. Their tastes were the same; they shared the same studies and the same recreations. In conversation it was curious to notice how one brother would begin a sentence and the other finish it, as if even in thought they were nearer to one another than two ordinary beings, and one mind knew intuitively the workings of the other.

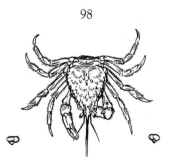

HARRY CLARKE

1889–1931

Often dubbed 'the outstanding Symbolist of Ireland', Harry Clarke was highly regarded as the greatest stained-glass artist of his generation.

Born in Dublin on St Patrick's Day (17 March) 1889, Clarke spent his adolescent years voraciously reading, drawing and studying graphic art, while training as a stained-glass apprentice. He soon became a supreme master of colour (influenced by his stained-glass work) as well as pen and ink illustrations; in retrospect it is unfortunate that his printed colour plates could never retain the wondrous incandescent power of his original paintings when reproduced and reduced to quarto size. 'Admirers of the artist's stained glass would scarcely recognise Mr. Clarke's jewels,' complained one critic of the published colour plates. But full justice was always done to his incredibly detailed and pungently atmospheric pen and ink illustrations, and these have rarely been excelled by any other artist.

For ten years (1915–25) Harry Clarke was commissioned to illustrate books exclusively for George Harrap, all produced in superb vellum, leather and cloth quarto editions. The best known of these are the two adult classics, replete with fantasy and horror, Poe's *Tales of Mystery and Imagination* (1919) and Goethe's *Faust* (1925).

Equally fine but somewhat gentler are Clarke's illustrations for two classic collections of fairy tales. *Hans Andersen's Fairy Tales* (1916) contained 40 full-page plates (including 16 in colour) and several decorative tailpieces. There is a magical combination of humour, drama and horror in these intricate and brilliant illustrations, seen to best effect in 'The Nightingale', 'The Little Sea Maid', 'The Tinder Box' and 'The Travelling Companion'. In the two illustrations of Great Claus and Little Claus, the latter character is a life-like self-portrait of Harry Clarke himself. *The Fairy Tales of Perrault* (1922) included 24 magnificent illustrations (12 in colour, 12 in black and white), with 21 decorations. Clarke's plates showing scenes from two of Perrault's best-loved stories – 'Cinderella' and 'The Sleeping Beauty' – are especially fine.

A major exhibition of Harry Clarke's work was opened by President Cosgrave in Dublin on 3 August 1925, and marked the peak of his career. One critic remarked on the opening day: 'Mr. Clarke's profusion is one of the most striking characteristics of his genius. The quantity of his work is scarcely less remarkable than its quality. The great artist always tends to be lavish with his gifts . . . The technique of all is equally impeccable.' Besides his graphic work, much of his stained glass and related material was also displayed.

By the late 1920s orders were flooding in for his celebrated glass designs, and his Dublin studio was renamed the Harry Clarke Stained Glass Studios Ltd. The intensity and long hours of his work led to agonizing headaches and a severe eye infection. He made periodic visits to a sanatorium in Switzerland for treatments of his recurrent tuberculosis, and eventually died there in January 1931, two months before his forty-second birthday.

100

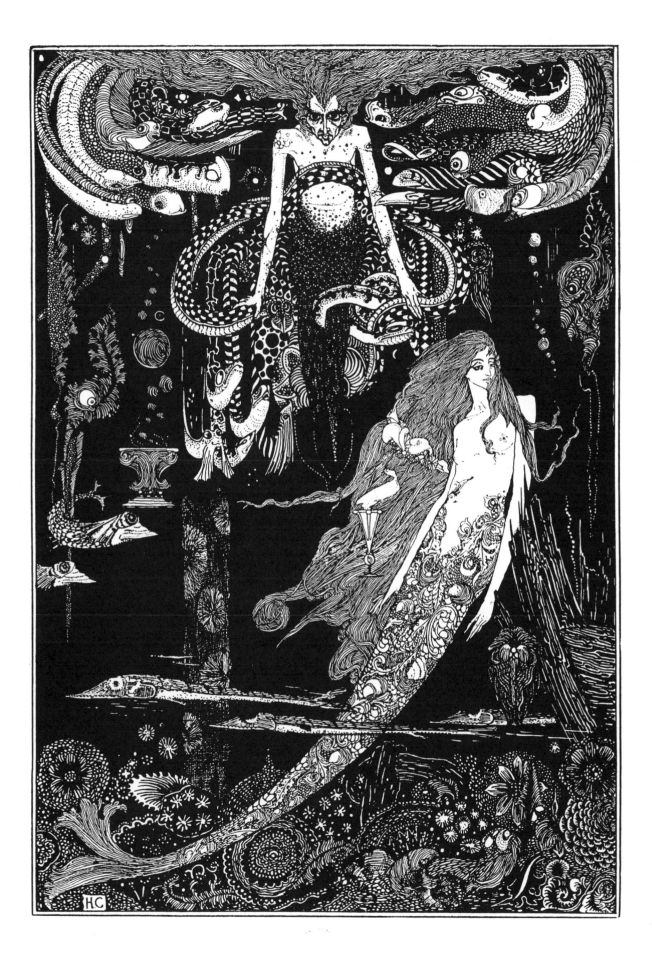

WILLIAM M. TIMLIN

1892–1943

The most original and beautiful children's book of the 1920s was William M. Timlin's masterpiece *The Ship That Sailed to Mars: A Fantasy*. Excelling the production values previously lavished on Willy Pogany and Harry Clarke, George Harrap published this huge and magnificent volume in November 1923, finely bound in quarter vellum richly decorated in gilt. 'Told and Pictured by William M. Timlin', the book contained 48 superb colour plates by the artist, alternated throughout with 48 leaves adorned with his fine calligraphic and poetic text. These pieces of art were all mounted by hand on grey matte paper, reminiscent of Harrap's best pre-war editions de luxe, notably Pogany's *The Rime of the Ancient Mariner*.

Timlin's fantasy is a magical combination of science fiction and fairyland. His watercolours equal the best work of Arthur Rackham and W. Heath Robinson, seen to great effect in 'The Raising of the Tower', 'The Celebration', 'The Palace Gardens', 'The Seven Sisters' (living in compact little moons, each complete with doors, windows and chimneys), 'The Jeweller's Shop' ('An elf would run out from some low-browed jeweller's shop and press a priceless ruby into his hand'), and 'The Temple' ('Myriad-pinnacled, with daring spans of flying buttress and airy bridge, a place of supreme happiness').

A total of only 2,000 copies of the book were produced in Britain, of which 250 were distributed in America by Stokes of New York (in 1924). They were sold for two guineas and twelve dollars each respectively. The film rights to the book were sold in America, but the movie, which was to be called *Get Off the Earth*, was never completed.

William Mitcheson Timlin was born on 11 April 1892 in Ashington,

102

Northumberland, the son of a colliery foreman. The family emigrated to South Africa in the early 1900s. After the First World War, Timlin became a successful architect based in Kimberley, where he died in 1943.

His later series of paintings, intended as plates for a book to be entitled *The Building of a Fairy City*, were never published in that form, but some (including the magical 'Fantasy and Triumphal Arch') have been issued as postcards in South Africa.

FRANK C. PAPÉ

1878–1972

Frank Cheyne Papé was born in Camberwell, south London, on 4 July 1878. As one of the busiest and most imaginative artists of the Golden Age, his career falls neatly into two periods: as a children's book illustrator before the First World War, and as a unique portrayer of 'cult' fantasies in the 1920s.

His earliest children's book illustrations, in Buckley's *Children of the Dawn* (1908) and Reader's *The Story of the Little Merman* (1909), were quite old-fashioned, in the nineteenth-century tradition, but his next commission showed Papé at his most inspired and inventive. Herbert Rix's fantasy, *Prince Pimpernel, or Kitty's Adventures in Fairyland and the Regions Adjoining* (1909), gave the artist free rein, in 8 colour plates and 34 black and white drawings, to display his gift for humorous and grotesque fantasy illustration, his chief speciality in the years to come.

Papé's illustrations for Hans Christian Andersen's *Fairy Tales*, John Bunyan's *The Pilgrim's Progress*, and *52 Stories of Classic Heroes*, all appeared in 1910.

He illustrated no less than ten books in 1911. Among these were revised editions of the *Strand Fairy Books* which had originally appeared with black and white illustrations by H. R. Millar in the 1890s; Papé now added 8 colour plates to each volume. In the same year Papé also contributed 12 colour plates to the new edition of George MacDonald's *At the Back of the North Wind* (with black and white illustrations by Arthur Hughes).

1912 was an equally busy year for Papé with commissions to illustrate several well-produced new children's books: Mrs Stawell's *The Fairy of Old Spain, and Other Important People*, Alfred Clark's *As It Is In Heaven*, F. W. Carove's *The*

FRANK C. PAPÉ

Story Without an End, and a large Christmas gift book, *The Book of Psalms*.

The war years saw two original compilations of folk tales by Richard Wilson, *The Indian Story Book* (1914) and *The Russian Story Book* (1916), each with 16 colour plates by Papé.

His last important children's book was an imposing new edition of Charles and Mary Lamb's *Tales from Shakespeare*, published by Warne in 1923. This contained 12 colour plates, with the customary large number of black and white illustrations, headpieces and decorations, features to be found in all the best-produced gift books.

By this time, Frank Papé had found his true métier thanks to the encouragement of John Lane at the Bodley Head. His bizarre and striking illustrations, imbued with black humour and eroticism, for the adult literary works of Anatole France, James Branch Cabell and François Rabelais, were critically acclaimed and overshadowed all of his earlier juvenilia. Cabell described Papé's drawings in *Figures of Earth* (1925) as 'opulent in conceits and burgeons and whimseys'.

After a splendid de luxe edition of Suetonius' *Lives of the Twelve Caesars* and a few minor commissions in the early 1930s, very little work came his way.

In 1938 he launched a series of illustrated paperbacks designed for very young children, *Composition Strips* – 'Picture stories to be fitted with words' – but this project collapsed after only one issue. His only regular work after this date was a long-running series of historical strip-cartoons for children which appeared in the American *Cleveland Plaindealer*. Unseen in Britain, these ran for many years until the artist's sight deteriorated. He died in Bedford in 1972 in his ninety-fourth year.

MONRO S. ORR

Monro Scott Orr was born in 1874, in Irvine, Scotland, the younger brother of artist Stewart Orr. He studied at Glasgow School of Art, and became one of Scotland's most popular book illustrators of the Golden Age.

His watercolour illustrations were always bright and vigorous, and often humorous in the style of René Bull and Charles Folkard.

Orr's books for children include *The Arabian Nights* (1913), *Grimm's Fairy Tales* (1914), *Mother Goose* (1915), and *The World's Fairy Book* (1930).

LAWSON WOOD

1878–1957

Lawson Wood was born in London on 23 August 1878, the son of landscape artist Pinhorn Wood. He studied at the Slade and Frank Calderon's School of Animal Painting. In his twentieth year, he became the principal artist of the C. Arthur Pearson group of magazines, and was a prominent member of the London Sketch Club. During the First World War, he served in France as an officer in the Kite Balloon wing of the Royal Flying Corps.

Wood was a fellow of the Zoological Society and (like Louis Wain) an active worker for animal welfare. Between the wars he was very well known for his humorous and animal watercolours and pen and ink drawings, especially those showing monkeys in comic situations, and many of these were reproduced as postcards. His most famous chimpanzee character, 'Gran'pop', was so popular that he was featured in a special Christmas Annual of his own.

Among Wood's own books are *Rummy Tales* (1920), *The Noo-Zoo Tales* (1922), *Fun Fair* (1931), *The Bedtime Picture Book* (1943), *Meddlesome Monkeys* (1946), *Mischief Makers* (1946), and a series of colour books. He also illustrated *The Bow-Wow Book* (1912), *Jolly Rhymes* (1926), and *The Old Nursery Rhymes* (1933).

Wood rebuilt and lived in a medieval manor house in Kent, before retiring to Devon where he died on 26 October 1957.

CHARLES FOLKARD

1878–1963

More than ten years before Mickey Mouse was created by Walt Disney, his British counterpart Teddy Tail – 'the Mouse in your House' – became the first newspaper cartoon animal to achieve worldwide fame. Charles James Folkard, Teddy Tail's creator, was equally well known for his wide range of colour plate illustrations, combining an infectious sense of humour with a wealth of fine detail.

Born in Lewisham, south London, on 6 April 1878, Folkard's early talent for drawing first became apparent while designing his own programmes for stage magic shows. He began contributing humorous drawings to *Little Folks* and the *Tatler*, and achieved his first breakthrough into the gift book market in 1910 with *The Swiss Family Robinson*. The beautiful drawings of flamingoes, monkeys, a walrus, a giant lizard, and the assorted livestock on the Robinsons' island, show the mastery of Folkard's technique when portraying animals and landscape in the fantastic world of imaginative illustration.

Pinocchio, the classic story of a wooden puppet which comes to life (first translated into English in 1892), was a perfect subject for Folkard's talents. His definitive edition, first published in September 1911 with a total of 77 drawings, including 8 watercolour plates, has been constantly reprinted up to the present day, delighting successive generations of readers. His characterization of Pinocchio follows the descriptions in Carlo Collodi's original text far more closely than the later Walt Disney cartoon film designs.

1911 also saw the production of two other Folkard classics: *The Children's Shakespeare* and *Grimm's Fairy Tales*. The latter was his first important commission for A. & C. Black, commencing a very busy and fruitful period of work for

CHARLES FOLKARD

that company over twenty years. Folkard's next books, all published by Black, were *Aesop's Fables* (1912), *The Arabian Nights* (1913) and *Ottoman Wonder Tales* (1915).

The plates in the latter volume were among his best, suggesting the jewelled illumination of old Persian manuscripts. His *Aesop* drawings of the hare and the tortoise, the owl and the grasshopper, and especially the country mouse and the city mouse, were clear precursors of his cele-rated characters which gathered in Britain's first daily newspaper strip to delight the readers of the *Daily Mail* in the grim early days of the First World War. *The Adventures of Teddy Tail* premiered on 5 April 1915 and achieved instant national popularity. Folkard named the mouse Teddy after his 3-year-old son, Ted. The exploits of Teddy, with Dr Beetle, the penny princess, grass-hopper, snail, frog, golliwog and all the others, were reproduced in a series of books running from 1915 to 1926

and include *Teddy Tail in Nursery Rhyme Land* (1915), *Teddy Tail in Fairyland* (1916), *Teddy Tail's Alphabet* (1921) and *Teddy Tail's Adventures in the A B Sea* (1926).

The success of Teddy Tail inspired most other popular newspapers to introduce a long line of new cartoon animals, notably Pip and Squeak (*Daily Mirror*, 1919) and Rupert (*Daily Express*, 1920), and countless others ever since.

After the war Folkard continued to illustrate a splendid array of children's books for A. & C. Black: *Mother Goose's Nursery Rhymes* (1919), *British Fairy and Folk Tales* (1920), Arthur Brook's *Witch's Hollow, or the New Babes in the Wood* (1920), *Songs from Alice in Wonderland & Through the Looking Glass* (1921), Dorothy Black's *The Magic Egg* (1922), Frances Browne's *Granny's Wonderful Chair, and Its Tales of Fairy Times* (1925), and the Polish story *The Troubles of a Gnome* by Zofja Kossak-Szczucka (1928).

His most impressive 1930s volume was *The Land of* ... *Nursery Rhyme* (1932), edited for J. M. Dent by Alice Daglish ... and Ernest Rhys. This book includes some very fine watercolour ... and gouache designs of Old King Cole, The Queen of Hearts, Ride a Cock-Horse, Sing a Song of Sixpence, and other favourites.

In his later years Folkard worked on several volumes in Dent's popular Children's Illustrated Classics series, including George MacDonald's *The Princess and Curdie* and *The Princess and the Goblin*, and a new edition of *Grimm's Fairy Tales* (all 1949), and Roger Lancelyn Green's anthology *The Book of Nonsense, by Many Authors* (1956). This last title contains one of Folkard's most imaginative studies, 'A Nonsense Miscellany', a seaside scene populated with Baron Munchausen, Struwwelpeter, and various characters from the rhymes of Edward Lear and Lewis Carroll.

Charles Folkard remained active to the end of his life, completing his last drawing – an illustration of children's nursery rhymes – only ten days before his death on 25 February 1963.

111

IDA RENTOUL OUTHWAITE

1888–1960

Folkard's leading Golden Age artistic colleague in the 1920s lists of A. & C. Black was Ida Rentoul Outhwaite. Already a household name in her native Australia, she reached her peak in Britain during the 1920s when her exquisite watercolours of brownies, elves and fairies became enormously popular.

Ida Rentoul was born near Melbourne on 9 June 1888, and she spent most of her life in that city. As daughters of an eminent theologian and professor at Melbourne University, both Ida and her elder sister Annie showed remarkable early artistic talents and began contributing fairy stories to local magazines in 1903. Their first published booklet was *Mollie's Bunyip* (1904), and several more followed, with Ida's delicate drawings accompanying Annie's texts. Ida married Grenbry Outhwaite in 1909, and their four children served as models for many of her book illustrations during the next twenty years.

Ida Rentoul Outhwaite's first outstanding collection was *Elves and Fairies* (1916), published in a beautiful limited edition of 1,500 copies, each signed by the artist. This was the first major Australian gift book to be compared favourably with the similar British editions de luxe published during the previous decade. The mounted plates, 15 in watercolour and 30 in black and white, were of exceptional quality, and the book was acclaimed by critics as 'a storehouse of delight for children in particular, and a picture gallery in itself'.

During an extended visit to England in 1920, Ida R. Outhwaite held an exhibition of her work in London, and began her fruitful association with A. & C. Black who published five large gift book productions of her fairy-world paintings over the next ten years.

The Enchanted Forest (1921), *The Little Green Road to Fairyland* (1922), and

112

The Little Fairy Sister (1923), with accompanying texts by her sister and husband, were all given the accolade of edition de luxe status, an honour bestowed on far fewer illustrators after the war than before. Ida herself wrote and illustrated two more children's books for A. & C. Black: *Blossom* (1928), the story of a little girl and an orphanage cat; and the entrancing *Bunny and Brownie: the Adventures of George and Wiggle* (1930). Her last drawings for Black appeared in Tarella Quin Daskein's *Chimney Town* (1934), a very amusing collection of four stories including the Australian fairy tales 'Janie of the Magic Shoes' and 'Here Come the Bears', describing the emigration of Goldilocks' three bears.

In the meantime she had another grand compilation of her illustrations, *Fairyland* (1926), published in a very expensive limited edition in Melbourne. Cheaper editions of this collection were later issued in New York (Stokes, 1929) and London (Black, 1931).

The Depression years saw an inevitable decline in the popularity and demand for Ida Rentoul Outhwaite's fairy subjects, though she continued to receive irregular commissions for books, magazines, postcards and calendars up to her death on 25 June 1960.

J. R. MONSELL

1877–1952

John Robert Monsell was born at Cahirciveen, County Kerry, Ireland, on 15 August 1877, the son of the Resident Magistrate. Unlike his sister, Elinor Monsell (who studied at the Slade, and later illustrated the children's books of Bernard Darwin), he had no formal art training. He loved inventing stories for children and illustrated them in sketchbooks. This led to his first picture book, *The Pink Knight* (published in 1901 by Chatto & Windus), followed by several more, *Funny Foreigners*, *The Jingle Book*, and *Notable Notions* (all 1905).

He was soon established as one of the best humorous illustrators for children, and contributed to several magazines including *Little Folks*. His delightful sketches abound in the pages of Arthur Mee's *Children's Encyclopaedia*, and his illustrations enlivened several jolly books of the Edwardian era, including Eustace Miles and E. F. Benson's *Mad Annual* (1903), T. W. H. Crosland's *The Motor Car Dumpy Book* (1904) and M. C. Hime's *The Unlucky Golfer, His Handbook* (1904).

One of his most successful children's books was the edition of Thackeray's *The Rose and the Ring* (1911). Among the other books he illustrated were Compton Mackenzie's *Kensington Rhymes* (1912), Bernard Darwin's *Elves and Princes* (1913), Orlando Williams' *Three Naughty Children* (1922) and Laurence Housman's *What-o'Clock Tales* (1932). Monsell himself wrote and illustrated *The Hooded Crow* (1926), *Un-Natural History* (1936), and *Balderdash Ballads* (1934; with rhymes and music). In 1935 his operetta based on Sheridan's *The Rivals*, for which he had designed the sets and written the songs and music, was produced at the Embassy Theatre. He also designed the distinctive heraldic jackets for the historical novels of his wife Margaret Irwin, whom he married in 1929.

His last years were spent in Rye, Sussex, where he died on 20 March 1952.

JOHN HASSALL

1868–1948

John Hassall was extremely versatile in all corners of the artistic world: cartoons, advertising, watercolour and oil painting, besides a very large number of illustrated books. Having studied at Antwerp Art School and in Paris at the Académie Julien, he enjoyed great success and demand for his work ranging from cartoons in *Punch* to paintings at the Royal Academy.

He achieved his greatest fame as the 'Poster King' of Britain, early efforts for Colman's Mustard, Nestlé's Milk and Moonlight Soap leading to his most famous posters, 'I bet that's a Veritas' and the immortal 'Skegness Is So Bracing'.

He was elected President of the London Sketch Club in 1903, and was a close friend of Phil May, René Bull and Cecil Aldin. With Aldin he illustrated the large picture book *Two Well-Worn Shoe Stories* (1899), containing 'The Old Woman who lived in a Shoe' (Hassall) and 'Cock-a-doodle-do' (Aldin).

Among the many other children's books Hassall illustrated were *Grimm's Fairy Tales* (1902), *The Pantomime ABC* (1902), *The Old Nursery Stories and Rhymes* (1904), S. Hamer's *The Princess and the Dragon* (1908), W. C. Jerrold's *Mother Goose's Nursery Rhymes* (1909), Perrault's *The Sleeping Beauty and Other Tales* (1912), *Blackie's Popular Fairy Tales* (1921), *Blackie's Popular Nursery Rhymes* (1921) and *Blackie's Popular Nursery Stories* (1931), all very colourful and reflecting the artist's own bright and energetic personality.

John Hassall was always a cheerful, jaunty, larger-than-life character (like many of the subjects of his drawings) and loved collecting everything unusual from an Elizabethan four-poster bed to an American Indian head-dress and a copy of Napoleon's death-mask which he kept in his studio.

He designed the cover of the popular boys' magazine *The Captain* and the editorial figure of 'The Old Fag' which became a standard feature every month. His drawings also appeared in *The Boy's Own Paper*, *The Happy Annual*, *Judy*, *Little Folks*, *Pick-Me-Up*, *St. Paul's* and many other magazines.

An enormously popular and generous man, John Hassall died in his eightieth year in 1948. He was the father of writer Christopher Hassall and wood engraver Joan Hassall.

CECIL ALDIN

1870–1935

Mickey the Irish Wolfhound and Cracker the Bull Terrier were two of the best-loved canines to be found in children's books of the Golden Age, thanks to their owner Cecil Aldin, who delighted his public with many portraits of his dogs caught in comically appealing poses.

Born in Slough on 28 April 1870, Cecil Charles Windsor Aldin studied at Frank Calderon's School of Animal Painting, and achieved early success both as a poster designer and a comic illustrator. He was the first artist to illustrate Kipling's *Jungle Stories* for the *Pall Mall Budget* in 1894–5. His early book illustrations appeared in *Everyday Characters* (1896), *Prehistoric Man and Beast* (1896), *Two Little Runaways* (1898), and *Two Well-Worn Shoe Stories* (1899) with his friend John Hassall. The two artists were prominent members of the London Sketch Club, and also collaborated on the *Happy Annual* (1907).

From first-hand knowledge as a Master of Foxhounds, he conveyed his sense of humour and hearty personality in producing hundreds of coaching and sporting prints, and definitive illustrations for *The Pickwick Papers* (1910) and *Handley Cross* (1911–12).

His work for children included several picture books, notably *Black Beauty* (1912) and *Bunnyborough* (1919), but his many dog books proved to be the most popular of all. *A Dog Day* (1902) was 'exceptionally life-like and charming – a model of tense humour' (said *Punch*) and the first edition sold out very quickly. *A Gay Dog* (1905) was a bulldog who followed the pursuits of the 'smart set' and had adventures at Henley, Ascot, etc. Among his other most successful books were *The Snob* (1904), *The Black Puppy Book* (1904), *Ten Little Puppy Dogs* (1905), *Dogs of War* (1906), *Mac* (1912), *Mongrel Puppy Book* (1912), *My Dog* (1913),

CECIL ALDIN

Cecil Aldin's Merry Party (1913), *A Dozen Dogs or So* (1928), *Sleeping Partners* (1929) and the *Cecil Aldin Book* (1935). Aldin's dogs also made their appearance in nearly all his posters, from Colman's washing blue to Cadbury's cocoa.

He published his entertaining autobiography *Time I Was Dead* in 1934, and died shortly after on 6 January 1935.

LOUIS WAIN

1860–1939

While Cecil Aldin specialized in dog illustrations, and Lawson Wood attracted a large public with his humorous paintings of monkeys, Louis Wain reigned supreme as the most famous and popular cat artist of all time. His cats inhabit a comfortable domain which closely reflects the flamboyance and style of the Edwardian age. They wear top hats and monocles, give tea parties, play tennis, and take holidays at the seaside. For decades all cat lovers have found them absolutely irresistible. 'Louis Wain', said H. G. Wells, 'invented a cat style, a cat society, a whole cat world.'

Louis Wain was born in Clerkenwell, north London, on 5 August 1860. He attended the West London School of Art for three years, and had his first drawing (of bullfinches) published in a Christmas magazine in 1880.

His obsessive fondness for cats began when he frequently made sketches of 'Peter', his ailing wife's pet kitten and bedside companion. 'He became my principal model and pioneer of my success,' Wain wrote. 'He helped me wipe out, once and for all, the contempt in which the cat had been held in this country.' *Madame Tabby's Establishment* (1886) was the first of many books he illustrated.

A large number of his cat drawings appeared in the *Illustrated London News*, but the familiar and universally known version of the 'Louis Wain Cat', humanized and clothed, did not materialize until the Christmas issue of 1890 when 'A Cat's Party' was published. In that same year he was made President of the National Cat Club, and became a long-standing member of the leading animal protection societies, including Our Dumb Friends Leauge, Shelters for Stray Animals, and the National Antivivisection Society.

120

LOUIS WAIN

The first *Louis Wain Annual*, profusely illustrated by the artist, appeared in 1901, and his other books included *Pussies and Puppies* (1899), *Nursery Book* (1902), *Baby's Picture Book* (1903), *Kitten Book* (1903), *In Animal Land* (1904), *Animal Show* (1905) and *A Cat Alphabet* (1914).

Books by other authors which he illustrated were Morley's *Peter, a Cat o' One Tail* (1892), Father Tuck's *Pa Cats, Ma Cats and Their Kittens* (1902), Bingham's *Kittenland* and *Ping-Pong* (both 1903), Aldin's *Cat Tales* (1905), Hannon's *The Kings and the Cats* (1908), Woodhouse's *Cats at Large* (1910) and *Two Cats at Large* (1911), Pope's *The Cat Scouts* (1912), and *Cinderella and Other Fairy Tales* and *Little Red Riding Hood and Other Tales* (1917).

Louis Wain's books, annuals, picture postcards, china Futurist mascot cats, toys and sundry memorabilia were seasonal bestsellers as 'Christmas without one of his clever-catty pictures would be like a Christmas pudding without currants'. He was equally popular in America, where he received a great reception in 1907, and accepted a three-year contract to draw a cat strip-cartoon for the *New York American*.

Returning to England, Wain suffered from concussion after falling from a bus platform, and this accident is assumed to be the main factor contributing to the mental illness and schizophrenia which afflicted him during his last twenty years. He continued to draw and paint during his residence at the Royal Bethlem Hospital and Napsbury, near St Albans, and died on 4 July 1939.

L. LESLIE BROOKE

1862–1940

Leslie Brooke was, alongside Beatrix Potter, one of the two greatest and brightest jewels in the crown of Frederick Warne, publisher of the most successful and beloved animal tales and illustrations of the twentieth century.

Born in Birkenhead on 24 September 1862, Leonard Leslie Brooke studied art at the Royal Academy School in London and became a portrait painter of some distinction. He illustrated several children's books for Blackie, Dent and Cassell before succeeding Walter Crane as Mrs Molesworth's regular illustrator (eight books running from *Nurse Heatherdale's Story*, 1891, to *Miss Mouse and Her Boys*, 1897). The artist was always credited in his books as 'L. Leslie Brooke', or simply 'L.L.B.' on the drawings themselves.

His long association with the Warne imprint began in 1897 with his very successful black and white illustrations for *The Nursery Rhyme Book*, edited by Andrew Lang.

Brooke's painstaking draughtsmanship was seen to wonderful effect in his illustrated edition of Edward Lear's *Nonsense Songs*, published in 1900 as *The Jumblies* and *The Pelican Chorus*. His characterizations of 'The Dong with the Luminous Nose' and 'The Duck and the Kangeroo' are especially memorable. Quickly accepted as one of the definitive editions of Lear's verse, *Nonsense Songs* was reprinted many times, with freshly printed plates of Brooke's paintings installed for the new edition in 1954.

Inspired by Lear's humour to compose his own rhymes, Brooke created a charming new fantasy world for children in *Johnny Crow's Garden* (1903), based

123

on a rhyming game that he had played as a child with his father and brothers. He first heard of Johnny Crow from his father, and the artist's own picturesque garden at Harwell (in Berkshire) provided further inspiration as the setting of the bird's adventures, which were continued in *Johnny Crow's Party* (1907). This was another great favourite with children, again showing Brooke's inimitable flair for animal drawing and expression.

'Leslie Brooke's Little Books', each issued in pictorial boards with 8 colour plates and several black and white drawings, rivalled H. M. Brock's similar 'Fairy Library' series in popularity. Children everywhere delighted in Brooke's

124

L. LESLIE BROOKE

comical pigs, bears, lion and unicorn, and all the
other animals, usually seen upright with merry
twinkling eyes, in *The History of Tom
Thumb* (1904), *The Story of the Three
Little Pigs* (1905), *The Story of the
Three Bears* (1905), *The Golden
Goose* (1905), *Oranges and Lemons*
(1913), *The Man in the Moon* (1913),
This Litle Pig Went to Market (1922)
and *Little Bo-Peep* (1922). They were
also available in two handsome volumes,
The Golden Goose Book (1905) and *Ring o'Roses*
(1922). His artwork in these eight nursery rhymes and the
Johnny Crow books, full of deft touches of subtle humour, demonstrated that Leslie
Brooke was one of the most gifted and leading animal illustrators of his generation.

Other Warne collections of old fairy stories, *The House in the Wood* (1909),
The Truth about Old King Cole (1910) and *The Tailor and the Crow* (1911) were
equally popular. *A Roundabout Turn* by Robert H. Charles, the tale of a toad
wishing to see the world, was published with Leslie Brooke's drawings in 1930.
His last book, *Johnny Crow's New Garden* (1935), was dedicated to his grandson
Peter Brooke (recently Chairman of the Conservative Party and Secretary of
State for Northern Ireland).

L. Leslie Brooke died in Hampstead on 1 May 1940. His son Henry
(Home Secretary in Macmillan's Government) honoured his
father's life and work in *Leslie Brooke and Johnny Crow* (1982).

BEATRIX POTTER

1866–1943

Over the past ninety years, millions of children have grown up with the endearing pictures and stories of Beatrix Potter, delighting in the escapades of Peter Rabbit, Jeremy Fisher, Squirrel Nutkin, Jemima Puddle-duck, Mrs Tiggy-Winkle, and all the other lovable creatures of her imagination.

Helen Beatrix Potter was born on 6 July 1866 at the family home in Bolton Gardens, Kensington, London. She led a solitary childhood in a prosperous, typically Victorian family, and from an early age she was devoted to animals and drawing and painting. She kept many small pets in her nursery – including mice, a hedgehog, and rabbits – and made countless highly accurate drawings of flowers, plants and animals.

In her early twenties she owned a prize rabbit named Benjamin, but her greatest inspiration came from another rabbit, bought in Shepherd's Bush for 4s 6d, which she named Peter. *The Tale of Peter Rabbit* first took shape in the form of a long letter to a child friend, illustrated with pen and ink drawings. Further adventures were created in several more letters. A number of years later she redrew *Peter Rabbit* as a complete manuscript but, unable to interest any publishers in her work, she had 250 copies privately printed with black and white illustrations in December 1901, followed by another 200 (with a slightly amended text) in February 1902.

Frederick Warne now became interested in publishing the book, and 8,000 copies with colour illustrations were released to the general public in October 1902. Within a year, *The Tale of Peter Rabbit* attained six printings, with over 50,000 copies sold. *The Tailor of Gloucester* (also originally printed privately, in 1902) and *The Tale of Squirrel Nutkin* were both published by Warne in 1903 to

126

meet the phenomenal public demand for new Potter books. *The Tale of Benjamin Bunny* (1904) and *The Tale of Two Bad Mice* (1904) were both bestsellers; *The Tale of Mrs Tiggy-Winkle* sold 30,000 copies within a few weeks of publication.

Norman Warne, the youngest of the Warnes, was her editor, and during the course of their work together he and Beatrix developed a close friendship. In 1905 he proposed marriage, and Beatrix accepted, despite the hostility of her parents to her 'marrying into trade'. Tragically, Norman Warne died just three months later, of leukaemia. Beatrix Potter threw herself into her writing, and over the next eight years she produced a further thirteen books, forming the major body of her work.

In 1905, determined to establish some independence from her family, Beatrix had bought Hill Top, a farm in the Lake District, where she spent as much time as was permissible for an unmarried daughter. In 1909 she bought a second farm. A local lawyer named William Heelis advised her on the purchase and after several years he proposed to her. Once again, her parents objected to the match, but in 1913, at the age of 47, Beatrix Potter married William Heelis and no longer felt the need to write, devoting herself to her husband and her farms as she had previously done to her work. Her marriage marked the beginning of a new career as a farmer and sheep-breeder, and the books were now few and relatively unimportant.

When Beatrix Potter died some thirty years later, on 22 December 1943, she bequeathed her farmhouse and all her land (some 4,000 acres) to the National Trust.

In 1987 Warne reissued *The Tale of Peter Rabbit* and her other classic stories in a completely new edition, printing the illustrations from the original watercolours so that they were clearer and fresher than ever before.

128

MONRO S. ORR

plate 34

CHARLES FOLKARD

plate 35

JOHN HASSALL

plate 36

BEATRIX POTTER

plate 37

Opposite:

H. WILLEBEEK LE MAIR

plates 38 and 39

LOUIS WAIN

plate 40

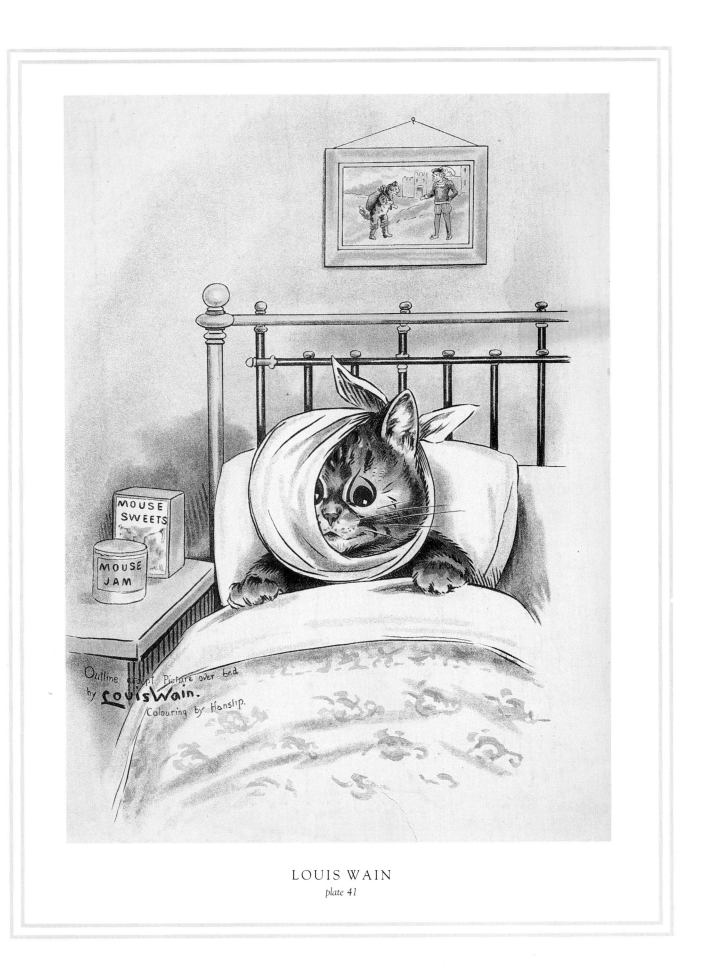

LOUIS WAIN

plate 41

L. LESLIE BROOKE

plate 42

L. LESLIE BROOKE

plate 43

The King of Hearts
    Called for those tarts
And beat the Knave full sore,

The Knave of Hearts
    Brought back those tarts
And vowed he'd
        steal no more.

MABEL LUCIE ATTWELL

plate 44

LAWSON WOOD

plate 45

ANNE ANDERSON

plate 46

ANNE ANDERSON

plate 47

GEORGIE-PORGIE.

MARGARET TARRANT

plate 48

MARGARET TARRANT

plate 49

E. H. SHEPARD

plate 50

MILLICENT SOWERBY

1878–1967

Amy Millicent Sowerby, daughter of the illustrator John G. Sowerby, became one of the most popular Edwardian postcard artists with her picturesque scenes from Shakespeare, and Kate Greenaway girls, and later she designed 30 sets for the perennial 'Postcards for the Little Ones' series. Her pictures of happy, rosy-cheeked children, and cheerful nursery themes sold in their thousands.

She was one of several artists commissioned to illustrate *Alice in Wonderland* (others included Arthur Rackham and Charles Robinson) when the book went out of copyright in 1907. Stevenson's *A Child's Garden of Verses* (1908), *Grimm's Fairy Tales* (1909), and *Little Stories for Little People* (1910), followed in quick succession.

Beginning in 1906 she illustrated a large number of children's books by her sister Githa Sowerby (*Children, Yesterday's Children, The Wise Book, The Merry Book, The Pretty Book, The Dainty Book, The Bright Book, The Bonny Book, The Darling Book*, and others), a very happy literary and artistic partnership which flourished for more than twenty years.

Millicent Sowerby remained an active watercolourist and flower painter at her South Kensington studio well into her eighties.

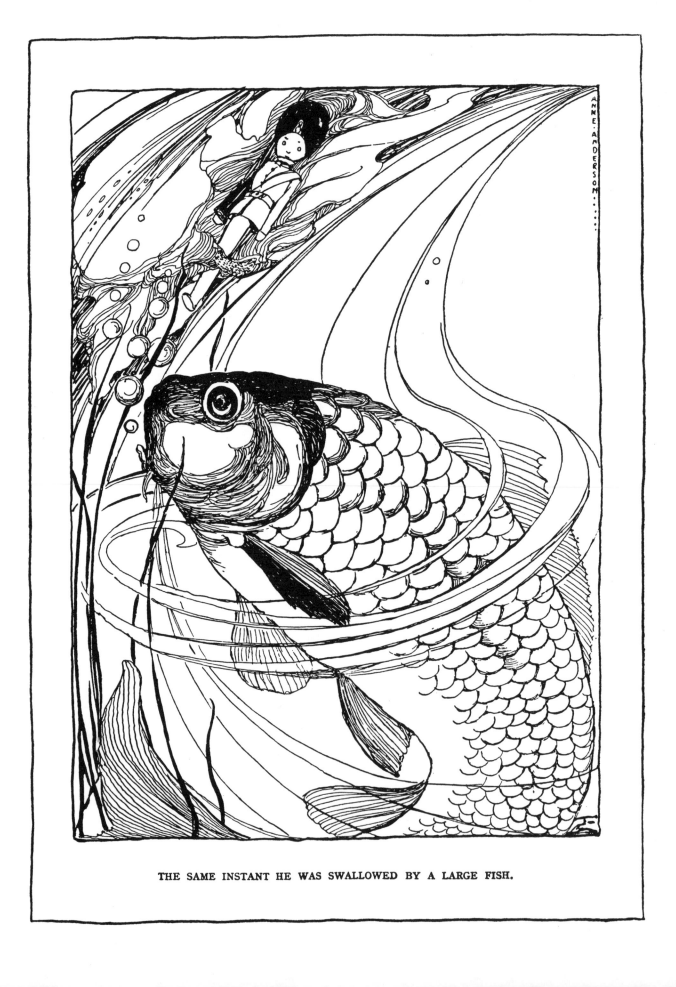

THE SAME INSTANT HE WAS SWALLOWED BY A LARGE FISH.

ANNE ANDERSON

1874–1930

Anne Anderson was born in 1874, and spent much of her childhood in the Argentine. In 1912 she married the painter Alan Wright and they collaborated on several children's books, often working on the same drawings together. Among these were *The Busy Bunny Book* (1916), *The Bold Sportsmen* (1918), *The Cuddly Kitty* (1926) and *The Podgy Puppy* (1927). On her own she wrote and illustrated a number of much-liked picture books including *The Funny Bunny ABC* (1912) and *The Patsy Book* (1919).

After the war she blossomed into one of the busiest and most consistently popular illustrators for children, following in the style and tradition of Charles Robinson and Jessie M. King. She was equally proficient in watercolour and black and white line artwork, and also designed greetings cards.

Among the many books she illustrated are Ethel Eliot's *The House Above the Trees* (1921), Agnes Herbertson's *Sing-Song Stories* (1922), Madeleine Barnes's *Fireside Stories* (1922), Charles Kingsley's *The Water Babies* (1924), Hans Andersen's *Fairy Tales* (1924), Johanna Spyri's *Heidi* (1924), and *The Old Mother Goose Nursery Rhyme Book* (1926).

MABEL LUCIE ATTWELL

1879–1964

Of all the popular illustrators who specialized in drawing children, only Mabel Lucie Attwell has remained a familiar household name to the present day. Her sketches and paintings of chubby children, invariably 2 or 3 years old, in books and the illustrated weeklies, appealed equally to everyone from members of the royal family and nannies and their charges, to young soldiers in the trenches during the First World War.

Mabel Lucie Attwell was born in Mile End, London, on 4 June 1879, and studied at Heatherley's and St Martin's School of Art. Like other imaginative artists, she quickly became bored by copying objects in the studio, preferring to illustrate her own fantasies. In 1905 she began illustrating several children's books by May Baldwin, Mrs Molesworth, Mabel Quiller-Couch, and other Chambers authors, usually providing 4 or 8 colour plates for each volume.

Three years later she married the artist Harold Earnshaw, and their daughter Peggy was destined to achieve immortality as the definitive 'Mabel Lucie Attwell toddler' in countless picture books and postcards. Married life saw the dawning of Mabel Lucie Attwell's greatest period of illustration with a high increase in quality commissions. For Cassell she illustrated *Grimm's Fairy Tales* (1910) and *Fairy Tales, Stories and Legends* (1910); and a fruitful association with the publisher Raphael Tuck brought *Old Rhymes* (1909), *Mother Goose* (1910), *Alice in Wonderland* (1911), *Grimm's Fairy Stories* (1912), *Our Playtime Picture Book* (1913), *Hans Andersen's Fairy Tales* (1914), *The Water Babies* (1915), *Children's Stories from French Fairy Tales* (1917), and *Baby's Book* (1922). Several individual tales from these books, especially those by Andersen and Grimm, were reissued separately by Tuck in the 1920s and 1930s.

132

She also illustrated two handsome gift books for Hodder & Stoughton, *Peeping Pansy* (1918) by Marie, Queen of Roumania (who invited Mabel Lucie Attwell to stay at the Royal Palace at Bucharest), and *Peter Pan and Wendy* (1921). The author J. M. Barrie admired her work greatly and personally requested her to illustrate this edition.

By this time Mabel Lucie Attwell was known nationally through her paintings and posters of children which were often accompanied by humorous verses and captions commenting on topical matters with a pithy but cheerful sentimentality. A huge industry of china, textiles, toys, 'Diddums' and 'Snookums' dolls, moneyboxes, needles and silk outfits, and postcards (mainly printed and published by Valentine & Sons of Dundee) grew from the public's insatiable appetite for any ephemera connected with Mabel Lucie Attwell.

The Lucie Attwell Annual was launched in 1922 and survived over half a century, with occasional title-changes to *Lucie Attwell's Children's Book* (1927–32) and *Lucie Attwell's Annual* (1933–74). During this period her loyal publishers were Partridge (1922–32) and Dean (1933–74), who issued a very large range of 'Lucie Attwell Picture Books' including *Tales for Bedtime*, *Wide Awake*, *Cuddle Time*, *Cutie Tales*, *Happy Day Tales*, *Great Big Budget Book*, and many others which often re-used stories and pictures from earlier annuals.

Sets of Mabel Lucie Attwell china were used in the nurseries of Princesses Elizabeth and Margaret, and later Prince Charles (a gift from the Queen in 1949).

Mabel Lucie Attwell spent her last twenty years in Fowey, Cornwall, where she died on 5 November 1964.

MARGARET TARRANT

1888–1959

Another very successful artist who supplied the demand for prettiness with her pictures of fairy-like children was Margaret Tarrant.

Born in Battersea, south London, Margaret Winifred Tarrant was the daughter of landscape painter Percy Tarrant. She studied at Heatherley's School of Art, and followed her father's career as a book illustrator, launching an extremely prolific output at the age of 20 with the publication of Kingsley's *The Water Babies* (1908), followed by at least a dozen more in the next four years, including her own *Autumn Gleanings from the Poets* (1910), *Fairy Stories from Hans Christian Andersen* (1910), Charles Perrault's *Contes* (1910), and Robert Browning's *The Pied Piper of Hamelin* (1912).

Besides her many children's books, Margaret Tarrant's postcards, calendars and silhouette designs were enormously popular. The plates in her edition of *Nursery Rhymes* (1914) were reissued as 48 bestselling postcards. Reproductions of her best-known painting, 'The Piper of Dreams', sold by the thousand to decorate sitting-rooms around the land. Her religious paintings achieved a great following in the 1920s and 1930s, especially 'He Prayeth Best', depicting a shepherd boy kneeling on a hilltop.

Tarrant enjoyed a long and fruitful association with the Medici Society, who published many of her beautifully designed calendars, greetings cards and large prints ('Sea Joy' and 'Woodland Friends'), as well as several attractive books like *Rhymes of Old Times* (1925), Eleanor Farjeon's *An Alphabet of Magic* (1928), and Marion St John Webb's *The Magic Lamplighter* (1926).

Also in the 1920s, in collaboration with Marion St John Webb, she helped to popularize one of the most favoured nursery themes of the period, 'Flower

134

Fairies', in a long-running series (*The Forest Fairies*, *The Pond Fairies*, *The Wild-Fruit Fairies*, *The Orchard Fairies*, *The Seed Fairies*, *The Twilight Fairies*, etc.).

Among her other illustrated children's books are A *Picture Birthday Book for Boys and Girls* (1915), *Alice's Adventures in Wonderland* (1916), Rudolph's *The Tookey and Alice Mary Tales* (1919), *Our Day* (1923), *Mother Goose: Nursery Rhymes* (1929), *The Margaret Tarrant Birthday Book* (1932), *Joan in Flowerland* (1935), *The Margaret Tarrant Nursery Rhyme Book* (1944), and *The Story of Christmas* (1952).

Her health and eyesight deteriorated in the 1950s. She died on 28 July 1959, leaving her estate to twelve charities.

HONOR C. APPLETON

1879–1951

Honor Charlotte Appleton was another of the extremely successful and prolific women illustrators whose beautifully delicate and charming watercolours enhanced more than a hundred children's books between 1902 and 1950. Like Cecil Aldin, Lawson Wood and many other prominent artists, Honor Appleton received invaluable training at Frank Calderon's School of Animal Painting. While still a student her first two books were published: *The Bad Mrs Ginger* (1902) and *Dumpy Proverbs* (1903).

She illustrated many girls' school stories; classics by Blake (*Songs of Innocence*), Dickens (*A Christmas Carol*), Grahame (*Dream Days*), and others; new fantasy tales for children (*The Gingerbread Man*, *The Blue Baby* and *Epaminondas*); and gift book editions of the fairy stories of Andersen and Perrault, which were very highly praised. Reviewing *Perrault's Fairy Tales* (1912) and the 12 delightful plates by this artist, the *Bookman* critic declared that 'Miss Honor Appleton can draw children – and for children – like no other artist alive.'

Appleton's most universally popular illustrations were of the little girl Josephine and her entourage of friendly toys – Granny, Quacky-Jack, Big Teddy and Little Teddy, and all the others in her wonderful nursery – in Mrs H. C. Cradock's long series of picture story books which ran from *Josephine and Her Dolls* (1916) to *Josephine Goes Travelling* (1940). A later compilation, *The Josephine Miniatures*, appeared posthumously in 1953.

In the 1930s she illustrated dozens of adapted children's classics in a long series for Harrap, including *Alice*, *Aladdin*, *Ali Baba*, *Black Beauty*, *Jackanapes*, *King Arthur* and *Robin Hood*.

LILIAN A. GOVEY

1886–1974

Lilian Amy Govey was one of the most popular and highly regarded illustrators of children's books and postcards of the 1920s, following the tradition of Anne Anderson and Millicent Sowerby.

She illustrated several books for Harrap, Wells Gardner & Darton (under the pseudonym 'J. L. Gilmour', following a disagreement with this company), Dean (*Dean's Happy Common Series*; *The Book of Happy Gnomes*), Nelson (*The Old Fairy Tales*), and especially Humphrey Milford (*The Rose Fairy Book*; *Nursery Rhymes from Animal Lands*) who also employed her talents in several playbooks, Christmas annuals, and the 'Postcards for the Little Ones' series.

She spent most of her adult life in a remote Sussex cottage, where she became devoted to the study of local history, folk lore and spiritualism.

CICELY MARY BARKER

1895–1973

A close friend and soulmate of Margaret Tarrant, Cicely Mary Barker was equally well known for her Kate Greenaway-style illustrations of cute and beautiful children, and above all for the picturesque 'Flower Fairies' which dominated her career for exactly half a century from 1923 to her death in Sussex on 16 February 1973.

These began with the very successful *Flower Fairies of the Spring* (1923) and *The Book of Flower Fairies* (1927), and her many other books include *Beautiful Bible Pictures* (1932), *A Little Book of Rhymes New and Old* (1937) and *The Lord of the Rushie River* (1938).

Her painting 'The Darling of the World is Come' was purchased by Queen Mary.

H. WILLEBEEK LE MAIR

1889–1966

Henriette Willebeek Le Mair was born in Rotterdam on 23 April 1889, the daughter of a wealthy corn merchant. Her parents were both artists who also wrote verses for their daughter to illustrate. In 1904, when she was aged only 15, her first book, *Premières Rondes Enfantines*, was published in France. During her stay in Paris she received advice and training from Maurice Boutet de Monvel, the most successful French illustrator of the day, who had been greatly inspired by the works of Kate Greenaway, and had subsequently created the new look of the modern French picture book.

Six years later she opened an exclusive school confined to one classroom in her own home, and took the opportunity of using her pupils as models for her watercolour drawings. By this time she had developed a distinctive style, with painstaking attention to detail in portraying children and their surroundings.

From 1911 she created a series of nursery rhyme illustrations for the music publishers Augener in London (and McKay in America). These were published as *Our Old Nursery Rhymes* (1911), *Little Songs of Long Ago* (1912), and *Old Dutch Nursery Rhymes* (1917), and met with universal acclaim from critics and the public alike. The *Studio* critic wrote: 'Since the days of Kate Greenaway I know of no one who has caught so well the spirit of childhood as Miss Willebeek Le Mair.' Augener published several more books by the artist including two nursery rhyme collections, *The Children's Corner* (1914) and *Little People* (1915); six 'little nursery rhyme books', each containing 10 illustrations in colour: *Grannie's Little Rhyme Book*, *Mother's Little Rhyme Book*, *Auntie's Little Rhyme Book*, *Nursie's Little Rhyme Book*, *Daddy's Little Rhyme Book* and *Baby's Little Rhyme Book*; the selection *Schumann's Piano Album of Children's Pieces*; *Baby's*

Diary, with several colour plates, and elegantly bound in pink or blue cloth; and 11 sets of children's postcards (each set comprising a dozen cards). All her illustrations in these books and postcards soon became accepted as classics of nursery illustration.

In her youth she had spent eighteen months with her parents in Arabia, and this experience led to a great interest in Eastern philosophy and the religious experience of art. She adopted the name 'Saida' when she married Baron van Tuyll van Serooskerken in 1920. They were both converts to Sufism as taught by Inayat Khan, a religion of universal brotherhood and love, and spent the rest of their lives helping the poor and various charitable causes.

Her most sumptuously produced book was *A Gallery of Children* (published by Stanley Paul in 1925) with words by A. A. Milne. She also illustrated Stevenson's *A Child's Garden of Verses* (1926), and *Twenty Jakarta Tales* retold by Noor Inayat Khan (1939). The work that ultimately gave her the most pleasure was *Christmas Carols for Young Children* (1946), published in The Hague where she had settled with her husband.

E. H. SHEPARD

1879–1976

Ernest Howard Shepard is best known as the visual creator of Winnie-the-Pooh and Toad of Toad Hall, and also for his drawings for *Punch* which appeared over a period of fifty years. 'He was perhaps the best-loved illustrator of children's books since Sir John Tenniel,' stated his obituary in *The Times*. 'The Pooh drawings were his greatest triumph, perhaps because his own human and unassuming genius was so much in harmony with the tender facetiousness of his fellow contributors to *Punch*.'

Shepard was born on 10 December 1879 in London where he attended Heatherley's and the Royal Academy School. He received medals for drawing and painting from life, and exhibited his first picture at the Royal Academy in 1901.

During the Edwardian decade, he received several commissions from Thomas Nelson to illustrate colour jackets and black and white plates for their series of classics, including *Tom Brown's Schooldays* and *David Copperfield*. He began his long career at *Punch* in 1907 while continuing to illustrate children's books like Harold Avery's *The Chartered Company* (1915), with 6 colour plates, a Nelson companion volume to H. R. Millar's edition of E. Hobart-Hampden's *The Little Rajah*.

From 1915 he served three years in the Royal Artillery in France, Belgium and Italy.

It was due to the foresight of the *Punch* editor, E. V. Lucas, that Shepard was asked to illustrate some verses by A. A. Milne due to appear in that magazine: *When We Were Very Young* (1924). Their success was immediate and soon led to the immortal *Winnie-the-Pooh* (1926), *Now We Are Six* (1927) and *The House at*

141

Pooh Corner (1928). Children everywhere loved Pooh and Piglet, Eeyore, Kanga, Tigger and their animal friends right from the start.

Shepard's wonderfully spontaneous and lovely drawings continued to decorate a large number of children's books, including E. V. Lucas's *Playtime and Company* (1925), Georgette Agnew's *Let's Pretend* (1927), Eva Erleigh (Lady Reading)'s *The Little One's Log* (1927), and the *Punch* anthology *Fun and Fantasy* (edited by Shepard, 1927).

The artist's equally successful association with Kenneth Grahame began in 1928 with *The Golden Age*, followed by *Dream Days* (1930) and *The Wind in the Willows* (1931).

Shepard remained busy and vigorous for the rest of his long life, illustrating dozens of classics for adults and children. He wrote his own first children's books in his mid-eighties: *Ben and Brock* (1966) and *Betsy and Joe* (1967).

The Pooh Story Book (1967) contained new line-and-colour pictures by Shepard, and he also coloured his original line drawings for new editions of *Winnie-the-Pooh* (1973) and *The House at Pooh Corner* (1974). He died in 1976, the fiftieth anniversary of Winnie-the-Pooh's original appearance.

In describing Shepard's place in the history of English illustration, the art historian Bevis Hillier wrote: 'I see him as the end of a tradition, not the beginning of one. He is the last of the great Victorian "black and white" men.'

SELECT BIBLIOGRAPHY

Beare, Geoffrey. *The Illustrations of W. Heath Robinson*. Werner Shaw, 1983.

Beetles, Chris. *Mabel Lucie Attwell*. Pavilion, 1988.

Birnbaum, Martin. *Introductions*. Sherman, 1919.

Bowe, Nicola Gordon. *Harry Clarke, his Graphic Art*. Dolmen Press, 1984.

Bowe, Nicola Gordon. *Harry Clarke*. Douglas Hyde Gallery catalogue, Dublin 1979.

Brooke, Henry. *Leslie Brooke and Johnny Crow*. Warne, 1982.

Cope, Dawn and Peter. *Illustrators of Postcards from the Nursery*. East West, 1978.

Coy, Ludwig. *Maxfield Parrish*. Academy, 1974.

Crane, Walter. *An Artist's Reminiscences*. Methuen, 1907.

Dale, Rodney. *Louis Wain, The Man Who Drew Cats*. Kimber, 1968.

de Freitas, Leo. *Charles Robinson*. Academy, 1976.

Engen, Rodney K. *Walter Crane as a Book Illustrator*. Academy, 1975.

Engen, Rodney K. *Randolph Caldecott, 'Lord of the Nursery'*. Oresko, 1976.

Engen, Rodney K. *Richard Doyle*. Catalpa, 1983.

Gettings, Fred. *Arthur Rackham*. Studio Vista, 1975.

Heron, Roy. *Cecil Aldin, the Story of a Sporting Artist*. Webb and Bower, 1981.

Holme, Bryan. *The Kate Greenaway Book*. Warne, 1976.

Hudson, Derek. *Arthur Rackham*. Heinemann, 1960.

Johnson, A. E. *Lawson Wood*. Black, 1910.

Johnson, A. E. *W. Heath Robinson*. Black, 1913.

Kelly, Clifford M. *The Brocks*. Skilton, 1975.

Knox, Rawle (ed). *The Work of E. H. Shepard*. Methuen, 1979.

Larkin, David (ed). *Arthur Rackham*. Pan, 1975.

Larkin, David (ed). *Dulac*. Coronet, 1975.

Larkin, David (ed). *Charles and William Heath Robinson*. Constable, 1976.

Larkin, David (ed). *The Fantastic Creatures of Edward Julius Detmold*. Pan, 1976.

Lewis, John. *Heath Robinson – Artist and Comic Genius*. Constable, 1973.

Moore, Anne Carroll. *The Art of Beatrix Potter*. Warne, 1955.

Muir, Percy. *English Children's Books, 1600 to 1900*. Batsford, 1954.

Muir, Marcie and Holden, Robert. *The Fairy World of Ida Rentoul Outhwaite*. Black, 1985.

Nicholson, Keith. *Kay Nielsen*. Coronet, 1975.

Price, R. G. G. *A History of Punch*. Collins, 1957.

Robinson, W. Heath. *My Line of Life*. Blackie, 1938.

Schnessel, S. Michael. *Jessie Willcox Smith*. Studio Vista, 1977.

Smith, Janet Adam. *Children's Illustrated Books*. Collins, 1948.

Spencer, Isobel. *Walter Crane*. Studio Vista, 1975.

Spielmann, M. H. and Layard, G. S. *Kate Greenaway*. Black, 1905.

White, Colin. *Edmund Dulac*. Studio Vista, 1976.

White, Colin. *The World of the Nursery*. Herbert Press, 1984.